Best wishes and much
appreciation to Scott Everbech

Tom Clinnie

D1431145

Decently and In Order

ON BEING THE CHURCH
AS THE CENTURY TURNS

Selected Reflections of
PAMELA P. CHINNIS

President of the House of Deputies
of the General Convention
of the Episcopal Church
1991-2000

Compiled and edited by
Pamela W. Darling

So, my friends, be eager to prophesy,
and do not forbid speaking in tongues;
but all things should be done decently and in order.

—I CORINTHIANS 14:39-40

Decently and In Order

On Being the Church
as the Century Turns

Selected Reflections of

PAMELA P. CHINNIS

Forward Movement Publications

Cincinnati, Ohio

Forward Movement Publications

412 Sycamore Street, Cincinnati, Ohio 45202-4195 USA
www.forwardmovement.org
© 2000

Preface

Monday, July 15, 1991—Fifth Legislative Day

The Committee on Dispatch of Business moved a
  Special Order of Business to receive nominations
  for President of the House of Deputies.

Deputy Beers placed in nomination the name of
  Pamela Chinnis of Washington.

Deputy Crump of West Tennessee moved election of
  Pamela Chinnis by acclamation.

Motion carried. Elected by acclamation.

Pamela Chinnis addressed the House, stating how
  much her election means for all women. She
  expressed her gratitude to the House for their faith
  and trust.

The President presented the President-elect with
  the keys to the General Convention Office in
  New York

1991 GENERAL CONVENTION JOURNAL, P. 620

The end of a 206-year tradition came simply. A position held
only by men since first established in 1785 was now filled by
a woman—by acclamation. At the 70th General Convention
of the Episcopal Church, Pamela P. Chinnis became the fourth
lay person and the first woman to be elected President of the
House of Deputies. It was 21 years after the first regularly-
elected women were seated as Deputies. Co-education had
reached "the senior House."

House of Deputies President Pamela P. Chinnis with then Presiding Bishop Edmond L. Browning.

Dedication

FOR PAMELA P. CHINNIS

Perhaps it seems odd to dedicate a volume of Pam Chinnis's writings to Pam Chinnis herself, but there it is. She was, at least theoretically, unaware of this project, undertaken as part of the activities marking the conclusion of her term as President of the House of Deputies. Therefore, her self-effacing tendencies did not interfere with putting her name in as many places as I could!

Poring over thousands of pages of manuscript, addresses, articles and sermons in order to assemble this collection, I was struck again by the breadth and depth of her knowledge, and by her willingness to say what needed to be said regardless of the cost.

God was smiling on the Episcopal Church the day Pam was elected President of the House of Deputies. She is a woman of uncommon intelligence, courage and wit, wholly dedicated to the Episcopal Church as an agent of God's love and justice in the world. Working with her these past nine years has been an extraordinary grace and blessing.

Pamela W. Darling, Th.D.
Special Assistant to the President
House of Deputies, the General Convention

Contents

Introduction

ALL THINGS SHOULD BE DONE
DECENTLY AND IN ORDER

Pamela P. Chinnis is a paradox. In late 1985, she walked demurely in procession into the chapel at the General Theological Seminary, looking like a typical "church lady," all hat and gloves and propriety. She was not, in fact, wearing hat or gloves (she says she no longer owns any hats), but that was somehow the impression.

Then the time came for her to preach, to a congregation of seminarians and alums just concluding a week-long program on "Anglican Identity." The "church lady" took off her non-existent gloves and delivered a stinging indictment, detailing the many ways the church had failed its female members. The Episcopal Church might be very forward-looking about things like civil rights and racism, she said; but when it came to the place of women in it's life, patriarchy reigned. The church simply must come to understand the implications of the fact that it took both male and female to create the image of God.

It was a galvanizing performance, not least because her remarks were delivered with penetrating clarity, without once losing that demure "church lady" presence. How extraordinary that someone like this had just been elected Vice-President of the House of Deputies of the General Convention. She combined strong commitments and a fearless ability to articulate them with a genteel Anglican façade. Decently and in order. Quintessentially Anglican. No wonder she had been appointed chair of the Presiding Bishop's Committee for the Full Participation of Women in the Church.

"CHURCH LADY" RISES TO THE TOP

Her journey through the organizational maze of the Episcopal Church, from parish custodian of the United Thank Offering to the President's chair in the House of Deputies, has been marked by these twin realities: Pam Chinnis is a very proper church lady; Pam Chinnis is a firebrand not afraid to take the lead in addressing injustice wherever she finds it.

Fortunately for the Episcopal Church, her gifts and commitment to change have carried her further and further into the institutions of church governance. She is a firm believer in the political process as an orderly method for maintaining the church's life. She is committed to opening the doors, the windows, the structures of the church to all of God's people, even though that means risking the anger of some who think that including one must involve excluding another.

She has been willing to bear the burdens of being first, and of being a leader. As the "first woman" to do a lot of things, she is frequently patronized and trivialized, while at the same time expected to do everything absolutely perfectly so her performance as "token" will open doors for others.

She has learned to put up with constant pressure from individuals lobbying for personal or political gains. Some think her low-key approach and good manners signify weakness. They suppose that her pleasant demeanor means she'll do whatever they ask—and are surprised if she doesn't!

She learned what it's like to be always in the spotlight, to deal with reporters whose questions may go way out of bounds. (During one interview prior to the 1994 General Convention, she was asked what she would do about a hairdresser during the two weeks she would be in Indianapolis!) She has learned that every decision is sure to make somebody angry so there's no point trying to avoid the hard choices.

She has a wonderful style in the Presiding Officer's chair, where the "church lady" persona sometimes comes in handy. She listens intently to every word that is said, and with a thorough knowledge of parliamentary procedure is often able to suggest a way out of a procedural tangle, so the House can accomplish what it seems to want. She is fair. Sometimes she is very funny. When Pam Chinnis is in the chair the House relaxes, knowing it is in good hands. All things shall be done decently and in order.

MINISTRY OF COMMUNICATION

Communication has been a major element in her campaign to open up the Church's institutional structures. Early in her first term, she began a series of "Letters to Deputies and Alternates," to keep members of the House informed of issues and events, and to support preparations for the next Convention. This was judged so useful that its distribution was extended to bishops and members of the various commissions and committees reporting to Convention. For months before each Convention, she also wrote a column for *Episcopal Life,* to inform the whole church about issues and procedures.

Her orientation presentation to Executive Council at the beginning of the triennium was so helpful that she was soon asked to offer remarks at the beginning of each Council meeting. These addresses combined reporting and commentary on issues and events of the day with mini-tutorials on relevant aspects of the church's institutional structures and how they could serve its mission.

She has been invited to speak and preach on countless occasions—to diocesan conventions, provincial synods, women's gatherings, groups of laity and clergy, parishes, cathedrals, seminaries; to conferences on justice, sexuality, racism, HIV/AIDS, women's history, spirituality, thanksgiving. Audiences who didn't know her are delighted and amazed as the real Pam Chinnis emerges, decently and in order, from under the non-existent hat and gloves.

THE INTEGRITY OF
THE GENERAL CONVENTION

Throughout her presidency, she has been concerned about threats to the Episcopal Church's bi-cameral system of government, which insures that clergy and laity have a voice alongside bishops. She worked hard to raise the profile of the House of Deputies, and to encourage use of canonical procedures for dialogue and decision-making.

Sometimes it seemed an uphill battle. As conflicts over ordained women and homosexuality deepened, more and more people shied away from dealing with them at Convention. The House of Bishops, under growing pressure as controversy increased and the work of administering dioceses became more and more demanding, turned inward for mutual support. Many bishops had never even served in the House of Deputies, and their twice-yearly meetings fostered a sense that bishops alone understood and knew what was best for the church.

Afraid of schism should definitive decisions be made, many sought to avoid voting altogether. Evading the questions seemed to promise continuation of the fragile status quo. In the short run it is sometimes an effective strategy, but evasion is not a permanent solution. Pam Chinnis did much to streamline and improve the way the legislative process worked, and sought to educate people about using it to discover the Spirit's leading on difficult issues. Her experience in the House of Deputies led her to believe that

Episcopalians love their church, and will almost always rise to the occasion when a high standard of interaction is set before them.

These threads wind throughout the pages that follow. They are assembled from speeches, articles and other communications over many years. Excerpts (from which ellipses have been excluded as too distracting) are arranged chronologically within each chapter.

A brief resume of Pam Chinnis's vast experience follows here. Her story in her own words will be found in the final chapter.

Pamela Pauly Chinnis

Pamela P. Chinnis was elected Vice President of the House of Deputies at the 68th General Convention of the Episcopal Church in 1985, and President during the 70th General Convention in 1991—the first woman to preside over the House in its two-century history. She was re-elected without opposition in 1994, and again in 1997.

Pamela Pauly Chinnis was born in Springfield, Missouri, to a political family which included her uncle Dewey Short, who represented Missouri in the United States Congress for a quarter century. After graduating Phi Beta Kappa from the College of William and Mary, Chinnis followed her mother to Capitol Hill where both worked in congressional offices.

When family responsibilities interrupted her work in Congress, Chinnis channeled her professional energies into a variety of civic and educational activities, including service as the first woman President of the Society of Alumni of the College of William and Mary, and two terms as member of its Board of Governors. With her former husband and children, she became increasingly active in her parish, the Church of the Epiphany in Washington, DC, serving as its first woman senior warden from 1972-78, and again from 1990 to 1995. Serving in the parish women's group led to election as diocesan president of the Episcopal Church Women and Presiding Officer at the 1976 Triennial Meeting, as well as appointments and elections to other positions of lay leadership at every level of the church: member of the Washington Cathedral Chapter, Vice President of Province III, Chair of Venture in Mission, member and then vice-chair of Executive Council, chair of the Board of the Alban Institute, and service on numerous other governing boards and advisory groups, where her quiet wisdom and droll wit have earned both respect and affection.

As her children became increasingly independent, Chinnis's service took her further and further afield. She was delegate to the 1978 Faith and Order Commission of the World Council of Churches in Bangalore, India, the Partners in Mission consultation of the Nippon Sei Ko Kai, the Anglican Council of North America and the Caribbean Conference on Refugees in Belize. On behalf of Bishop Desmond Tutu and the South African Council of Churches she was one of four Anglicans to testify before the 1983 Eloff Commission of Inquiry in South Africa.

As a lay delegate to the Anglican Consultative Council, Chinnis participated in four of its triennial meetings, in Canada (1979), Singapore (1987), Wales (1990) and Capetown (1993). In 1988 she was part of the ACC delegation to the Lambeth Conference, one of only nine official women participants in that gathering, and served from 1987-93 on the Standing Committee of the Anglican Consultative Council. From 1988 to 2000, she also served on the General Board and Executive Coordinating Committee of the National Council of Churches. She was head of the Episcopal Church's delegation to the 8th Assembly of the World Council of Churches in Harare, Zimbabwe, in 1998, where she was elected to the WCC's Central Committee.

Chinnis's commitment to the inclusion of all baptized people in the full life of the church is long-standing. She was an early supporter of the movement for the ordination of women, a delegate to the International Consultation on the Community of Women and Men in the Church, in Sheffield, England in 1980, and chair of the Presiding Bishop's Committee for the Full Participation of Women in the Church from 1985-88. As President of the House of Deputies, she has exercised her responsibility as appointing officer to extend the diversity of those serving on policy-recommending commissions, committees, boards and agencies, as well as the legislative committees which handle resolutions during the General Convention itself.

Asked how she reconciles her forthright commitment to women's issues with the responsibility of the President to serve all Episcopalians, Chinnis says, "The president of the House of Deputies cannot be a single-issue person, no matter the issue. My commitment is to the inclusion of all people, regardless of their race or class or gender or sexuality. Sexism is only a symptom of the larger problem, which is injustice and oppression. That's one thing I've learned over the years: from an initial awareness of discrimination against women, I've grown to see the connections between racism, classism, sexism—all the differences which divide the people of God from one another. You can't be against discrimination against women and be for discrimination against anyone else."

A recipient of honorary degrees from the College of William and Mary, the General Theological Seminary, Virginia Theological Seminary, Berkeley Divinity School at Yale, the Church Divinity School of the Pacific, and St. Paul's College, Lawrenceville, Virginia, and the Distinguished Christian Service Award from Seabury-Western Theological Seminary, Dr. Chinnis still lives within sight of the U.S. Capitol in Washington, D.C. Her daughter Ann is an emergency room physician and professor of emergency medicine in West Virginia, and her son Cabell is a Washington attorney.

> *Executive Council members and others often
> expressed appreciation for President Chinnis's
> explanations of how the church works, how it got
> that way, and how that relates to its mission and
> the Christian responsibilities of its leaders. These
> "pastoral teachings" derived from her own
> extensive involvement in the Church and famil-
> iarity with Episcopal history. This "polity primer"
> was originally suggested by members of her
> Council of Advice.*

Church Governance Evolves

ORIGINS OF OUR CURRENT STRUCTURE

Wardens' Conference, Diocese of Virginia, March 15-17, 1991

We often hear it said that those who drafted the Constitution of the United States walked across the street, so to
speak, and drafted the Constitution of the Episcopal Church.

The Declaration of Independence not only severed our
connections with England, it also severed connections
between the American Anglican Church and the Church of
England. Try to imagine, if you will, an integral part of the

Mother Church of England suddenly and severely left to its own creativity, ingenuity and devices. The Church in the new Republic was little more than a collection of individual parishes without any central organization.

To understand the governance of the Episcopal Church in the USA, one needs to look at the pre- and post-revolutionary period. The ecclesiastical revolution was almost as significant as the civil revolution. From 1789 on, bishops and budgets were both brought forward by ballot, in all places including the General Convention, by clergy and laity meeting and voting together. This phenomenon was not only unique but revolutionary.

The Episcopal Church in America quite consciously determined to eliminate any use of the medieval concept of a magisterial prince-bishop, appointed by and responsible to the king. In its place they sought to recapture the primitive concept of the episcopate as wholly separate from the state and servants of the Church and not its lords.

THE BASIC UNIT

The greatest opposition to the episcopacy being established in the colonies emerged from those areas, especially in the South, where vestries and parishes were fairly independent, having been forced to carry on with few clergy, and with no bishops at all, since the establishment of the original colonies.

In Virginia, for example, the vestry selected the priest, wardens were the executives of the parish, and even raised a tobacco tax for church support. In the absence of clergy, they selected lay-readers to lead the congregation in worship. The powers of Virginia vestries over the clergy seemed to many a new and lasting and entirely satisfactory form of clergy-lay relationship. In New York, Pennsylvania, New Jersey and Delaware, the vestries could raise funds and select their priests, with or without tenure. As a result, the responsibility for the congregation's growth, health, and prosperity was primarily the responsibility of the laity.

The legal supremacy of the General Convention was built on a base of broad powers, granted, retained and exercised on the local and parish level, regardless of the theological concept that the bishop is the central focus and symbol of the unity of the diocese, and that the basic unit of the Church is the diocese. In the colonial period and even today many would contend, the basic unit of the Church was experienced at the parish level.

PROTECTING THE ROLE OF THE LAITY

One does not have to serve long in the House of Deputies until the clarion, "the integrity of the General Convention," becomes a banner under which Deputies serve, even though they may not know the historical reasons behind it. Bishops, and particularly a Presiding Bishop, with no service in the House of Deputies will forget that fact at their own peril. No more dramatic example of this principle exists than that of the 1973 General Convention, when concurrence with the House of Bishops' election of the Presiding Bishop led to a prolonged, intensive debate in the House of Deputies.

We have periodically had resolutions to General Convention calling for a change of the title of the Presiding Bishop to Archbishop. They have been rejected each time, and it is only very recently, as a result of our involvement in the Anglican Consultative Council, that we have taken to referring to the Presiding Bishop as "Primate," and using the title "Most Reverend" rather than "Right Reverend." Such developments must be carefully watched. ✠

THREATS TO THE BI-CAMERAL SYSTEM

St. Philip's, Laurel, Maryland, Fall 1991

It was the intention of our forebears that we should have a federal type of polity for the General Convention, that the two Houses should be equal, and that one House could not function or operate without the other. Paramount in this contract form of polity was the insistence that each constituency is represented by an equal vote and the center of authority is devolved over a number of individuals or their representatives. There was and indeed there still is a strong states' rights theory of polity with the General Convention. It is most readily seen when someone suggests a proportional representation of deputies based on the communicant size of a diocese. It would be surprising indeed if such a resolution were to receive a concurrent majority of both Houses.

Recently we have seen more and more the shift toward a highly centralized method of operating the church at the national level. There are a number reasons for this. Presiding Bishops have become more powerful; staff persons at the national level have assumed more and more authority, the General Convention, which how has a potential membership of close to 950, has been described as a beached whale where 30-45 deputies do most of the talking. With General Convention meeting only once every three years, deputies come together, deal with hundreds of resolutions, pass many without adequate background, and go home and forget about them.

BISHOPS ACT APART FROM CLERGY AND LAITY

Another dynamic in the increased centralization of church governance and the erosion of the integrity of the General Convention is the current practice of the House of Bishops to meet annually. Although they cannot act officially without the concurrence of the Houses of Deputies, there has been a tendency to forget that. As the historian, John Woolverton, said,

> *Today in the Episcopal Church in particular, and in the Anglican Church in general, there is a tendency to ignore the late eighteenth century lesson of American ecclesiastical democracy. This tendency is manifested, for example, in the action of the House of Bishops, taken apart from the laity and clergy of General Convention, in announcing a "conscience clause" for those clerics opposed to the legally approved ordination of women.*
>
> *Moreover, the increasing authority of the Lambeth Conference of Anglican Bishops, the move to have Anglican prelates meet bi-annually, apart from the clergy and laity of the Anglican Consultative Council, and the casual talk at Lambeth, 1978, of freeing the Archbishop of Canterbury from his diocesan and national responsibilities in England to become a sort of Anglican pope, all serve to show how little the lessons of the 1780's have been learned.*

It requires of each of us as members and leaders in this church that we take our responsibilities seriously, that we do our homework, and that we hold those elected to represent us accountable. The legislative process, and indeed the structure of the General Convention and the Church, begin and end for all practical purposes with the local congregation. If understanding and commitment are absent at this level, they won't be found higher up.

More and more we see efforts to increase the role and power of the House of Bishops and the national church staff. We have every right to be concerned. Eternal vigilance is the price of freedom from a church dominated by the House of Bishops.✠

Relationship of
Convention and Council
Executive Council, New York City, October 31, 1994

Fifteen years ago I attended my first meeting as a newly-elected member of the Executive Council, arriving in 1979 for the prescribed six-year term. In 1985, when my term had ended, Presiding Bishop Browning invited me, as the new Vice President of the House of Deputies, to sit on the Council with voice but no vote—an honor I enjoyed for six more years.

And then in 1991 I came here again in my own right, since the President of the House of Deputies serves as vice-chair of the Council. In that capacity, I have been blessed to work as a full partner with the Presiding Bishop, sharing in presiding over these meetings, participating in debate and decisions—some of which were tough ones—and working with him and the senior staff to implement Council decisions at the Episcopal Church Center.

This means that, since 1979, I have had the privilege of being part of five different Executive Councils. Each triennium we are born anew. Each Council has its own spirit and dynamics, each its own set of issues to address, each its own priorities and commitments, and even its own developing body of shared experiences, family jokes and camaraderie.

Why Are We Here?

The Executive Council was first created by the General Convention of 1919, to unify the mission activities then being carried out by separate boards and agencies. Canon I.4 says in part:

> *There shall be an Executive Council of the General Convention whose duty it shall be to carry out the program and policies adopted by the General*

Convention...and between sessions of the General Convention [the Council] may initiate and develop such new work as it may deem necessary.

We are, then, a creature of the General Convention, responsible for implementing its programs and policies, and accountable to the Convention for any "new work" we may deem necessary to the Church's mission. The General Convention, lest we forget, is the body to which our Constitution and Canons assign legislative authority over all that defines our corporate life:

- First and foremost, it is the General Convention that authorizes our liturgical texts and controls the revision process for the Prayer Book, which gives voice to our worship and embodies our theology.

- The Convention also determines the geographic areas which shall be dioceses of this Church, and who may be consecrated bishop, thus establishing the basic units of our institutional life.

- Convention adopts and revises the Constitution and Canons which govern us, elects people to carry out duties prescribed by the canons, and approves the collection and dispersal of funds to support the mission activities it has authorized.

Worship, membership, governance, program and finance—responsibility for all these elements of our life as Episcopalians resides with the General Convention, and with us as its Executive Council during the triennium. ☩

EXECUTIVE COUNCIL RESPONSIBILITIES

Executive Council, Bellevue, Washington, June 13, 1995

Three times a year, we come together as the Executive Council of the General Convention of this Church, "to carry out the program and policies adopted by the General Convention." The canon creating the Council was first adopted in 1919, and its key provisions were that the Council is to "have charge of the unification, development and prosecution of the Missionary, Educational, and Social Work of the Church," and to serve as Board of Directors of the Domestic and Foreign Missionary Society with "power to direct the disposition of the moneys and other property of the Society" *Canon I.4.1(a) & (g).*

In thinking about these responsibilities, I find it helpful to recall the context in which the Church decided to create the Council. Prior to 1919, the General Convention itself, meeting once every three years, was the primary element of what we now call "the national church." There was no centralized institution functioning as "the church" between Conventions.

The Domestic & Foreign Missionary Society employed a small staff to support the work of missionaries in various parts of the world. Working alongside the Secretaries of Domestic and Foreign Missions were Julia Chester Emery and her staff of the Woman's Auxiliary of the Society.

There was also a General Board of Religious Education, a completely separate entity providing resources for Sunday Schools and other Christian education programs. Joining these independent agencies in the old Bible House on Fourth Avenue in Lower Manhattan was the Social Service Commission, which Convention created to coordinate programs in labor relations, health and welfare, and related social ministries. Although these three programs shared space, their small administrative staffs, budgets, governing bodies, purposes and goals were all separate and uncoordinated.

The Council was created to replace the separate governing boards for those programs, to provide coordinated
oversight and administrative consolidation. As Chair of the
Council, the Presiding Bishop had ultimate executive
authority, but until 1943 the Presiding Bishop was also a
diocesan bishop whose ability to direct day-to-day operations
was quite limited. Similarly, the President of the House of
Deputies, Vice-Chair of Council, was usually engaged in
full-time ministry elsewhere.

Program staff are accountable to the Council, and used
to say of themselves "I work for the Council," but during the
Council's 75-year history there have been many different
arrangements for daily management and executive oversight
of the missionary, educational and social programs of the
Church for which we—as the Council—are ultimately
responsible.

FAITHFULNESS TO THE PAST
REQUIRES CONSTANT ADAPTATION

I rehearse a little of this history because I find it reassur-
ing. As a church we have always been engaged in modifying
our administrative structures to meet changing needs, to
adapt to the gifts of the particular individuals God calls as
our leaders at different times, and to respond to the weaknesses of structures or people as they become apparent.

We are in the midst of another cycle of adaptation now. It
is not very comfortable. In fact it's downright uncomfortable—unsettling, disorienting, challenging, frightening the
way being called into an unknown future is always frightening. But God has gathered us to serve as members of the
Council at this particular moment, and we can trust God to
provide the wisdom and courage to respond to our challenge
as our predecessors responded to theirs.

The Structures Supporting Our Mission

The Church has a number of structures for mission in addition to the Executive Council and staff of the Church Center. For some years now, awareness has been growing of the need to adapt, prune, modify, and generally renew many of those structures.

- The various committees, commissions, boards and agencies we refer to as "interim bodies," along with a relatively new category of "committees reporting to Executive Council," have proliferated over the years, as new issues have arisen in the life of the church which seemed not to fit within the scope of existing groups.

- Provinces and dioceses have waxed and waned in their ability to support Christian proclamation and service as populations have shifted, the economy has fluctuated, and leadership has changed.

- The General Convention itself became cumbersome as its size increased, and procedures which worked well for a smaller convention in the manual age have required substantial modification and streamlining. ✠

Structures—Re-Examining How We Work Together

Joint Meeting of "Interim Bodies", Minneapolis, Minnesota, October 12-14, 1995

There has never been a meeting quite like this before. The various interim bodies on which you serve, together with the Executive Council, are the national leadership of the Episcopal Church between General Conventions. However, our structures have compelled you to operate as leadership in diaspora, scattered, with little communication or coordination. Your work fits together efficiently only insofar as the directives given you by the General Convention are consistent and coherent, and the Holy Spirit who enlivens all our work is able to override our individual tendencies toward competition, empire-building and the like.

So the Presiding Bishop and I thought it might be time to call the diaspora together, so we can see and experience the interim leadership of the Episcopal Church, and together work at improving our institutional structures so they will better support our life as the people of God. My very greatest hope for this gathering is that it will develop our sense of community, here in this portion of Christ's Body that we call the Episcopal Church, so that we can corporately develop more effective ways of carrying out Christ's mission and ministry in our time.

MEMBERS OF THE DIASPORA

"Interim Bodies" is the clumsy term we have used for referring to the various committees, commissions, boards and agencies that function "in the interim" between Conventions. They are a motley lot, these groups. Some are enshrined in the canons. Some are authorized by Resolutions renewed or modified at successive Conventions. Some report directly to the Convention, while others report to Executive Council. Some have been charged with short-term tasks and naturally to go out of existence when those tasks are completed; others deal with longer-range matters that may deserve attention for a number of years; and a very few are virtually permanent units dealing with perennial aspects of our life as a church.

The most clear-cut are the canonically-mandated Standing Commissions, which are the primary study arm of the church, authorized to explore emerging issues and recommend policy to the Convention and, in urgent matters, to the Executive Council. The Council is empowered to oversee implementation of the policies adopted by the Convention, and to initiate new ones in the interim if circumstances require, chiefly through the programs under the direction of the Presiding Bishop, coordinated by the staff of the Episcopal Church Center, in New York and in field offices in Washington, Philadelphia, Oklahoma and Texas.

Our Church's structure has grown willy-nilly for two centuries. Organizational charts and diagrams illustrate the convoluted relationships between some of our units.

- The Committee on the State of the Church of the House of Deputies is the oldest by far, having been established at the second full meeting of the Convention, in 1792.

- Next in seniority is the Standing Liturgical Commission, set up in 1913, initially to produce the 1928 Prayer Book, and the Church Music Commission which came along in the midst of that revision process, in 1919.

- Human Affairs as we now know it was formed in 1958, as a reconfiguration of what had been called in the post-Depression era "Social Reconstruction," which I believe was itself successor to the earlier Social Service Commission, which succeeded the Committee on Capital and Labor at the turn of the century.

- Health formed in 1973, was then combined with Human Affairs for four triennia, and then separated out again in 1988, at the same time HIV/

AIDS became first a Joint Commission of Convention and later a Commission of Executive Council.

• The Structure Commission itself was formed in 1961 by combining committees of Deputies and Bishops, to look at the workings of General Convention and the Provinces. In 1967 its mandate was expanded to include the whole church, including the functions of the Presiding Bishop's office. Through its work, and that of its predecessor bodies, new groups have been formed and others discontinued. More than half of today's Standing Commissions took canonical form only in the 1970's and 1980's.

As these examples illustrate, there are good historical reasons for some of the anomalies in our current structures—but they are, for the most part, explanations, not justifications for a permanent status quo. We have always gone through cycles of organizational sprawl to accommodate changing situations and needs, followed by reorganization of responsibilities, pruning obsolete functions, and strengthening lines of communication and cooperation between the various components. ✠

> *In October, 1995, President Chinnis and Presiding Bishop Browning invited the committees, commission, boards and agencies reporting to the General Convention to meet in Minneapolis for several days. The agenda included individual group meetings, plenary sessions, common meals and shared worship. The Convocation was repeated in the next triennium, in early 1998.*

LESSONS OF MINNEAPOLIS

Executive Council, Birmingham, Alabama, October 31, 1995

The Minneapolis convocation gave me a tremendous feeling of optimism about our church, and immense gratitude to God for letting me be a part of this vital time in our history. Bishop Browning and I were able to visit more than half the twenty-four groups holding individual meetings during the conference. I was awed by the breadth and depth of the ministries God has given us to perform, and the extraordinary talent and dedication of people throughout the church engaged in those ministries.

It was a wonderful tonic, after months of dealing with the aftermath of the embezzlement and other internal concerns that pre-occupy us as designated leaders of the institution. I rejoice in this reminder that the primary energies and attention of the committees, commissions and other agencies of the General Convention which comprise "the national church" are directed, like that of our dioceses and parishes, toward the real work of the Gospel: proclaiming the Good News of Jesus Christ, ministering to the suffering, seeking peace and justice in the human family, exercising stewardship over God's creation.

I was struck by the widespread willingness to explore

new approaches to our work together, and the energy and enthusiasm that comes with that freedom. The frustration that followed the last Convention's inability to agree on how to reform our institutional structures seems to be melting away, and we are moving forward with a refreshing openness about possibilities and a willingness to experiment.

SEEKING NEW WAYS OF DOING BUSINESS

The participation of so many in the Minneapolis meeting was itself an example of that willingness to experiment. There had never been such a mid-triennium gathering. The Presiding Bishop and I invited interim bodies to meet together in part to facilitate the work of the Structure Commission, which was charged by the 1994 Convention to identify areas of overlap among the interim bodies with an eye to better stewardship of church resources. But Structure's task was only one part of the conference.

We were also experimenting with a new way of doing business: a more collaborative style of ministry based on personal contacts, networking, and a non-hierarchical, cooperative approach to policy development and program planning. By bringing people together physically, in one place, for several days of interaction, we hoped to stimulate a stronger sense of unity and coordination in our work, through awareness of links between tasks and better communication among groups in the future now that they've had a chance to meet face to face. The role of technology in networking was also apparent, as people exchanged QUEST inbox names and electronic mail addresses, and those who are not yet on-line heard pep talks and reassurance from those already at home in cyberspace.

Staff were efficiently deployed in Minneapolis too. Program people were available to many more groups than if they'd been meeting separately. The Convention office coordinated all the arrangements, and every group had access to computers, copy machines and staff support far beyond what is available when they meet alone. Although the schedule was intense and we were all tired by the end of it, most also indicated that the cross-fertilization of ideas was invigorating and their work got done in spite of the time-pressures.

NEW MODELS FOR MINISTRY

I review all this, not just so we can feel good about what happened in Minneapolis, but because what happened there holds so much promise. By organizing our common time around worship and fellowship over meals, we bore witness to ourselves and to others that our work on behalf of the institution is rooted in our life as a community of faith, that the whole is greater than the sum of the parts, and that through our common life God channels energy and creativity far beyond what we can generate individually.

In this era of apparently declining material resources, this reminder of God's ability to multiply our offerings is very timely. Minneapolis provides evidence of the importance of pooling resources through networking, to offset the increasing isolation and inefficiency fostered by old top-down models of organization.

THE CHALLENGE OF CHANGE

There are historical reasons for the anomalies in our current structures—but they are explanations rather than justifications for any permanent status quo. We have always gone through cycles of organizational sprawl to meet changing situations and needs, followed by reorganization of responsibilities and pruning obsolete functions.

This is part of our on-going task as stewards of the institutional church, to make the best possible use of our time and talents in carrying out Christ's mission, and to maximize the use of material and financial resources in support of that mission. The specific tools used in each generation—the patterns of organization, the communication technologies, the concepts and theological vocabulary we use in carrying out the church's mission—all necessarily change with the times.

I thank God that the Episcopal Church is facing boldly into the challenges of structural renewal in anticipation of a new millennium, despite the fears and resistances such a process inevitably elicits. As a wag has said, "Blessed are the flexible, for they shall not be bent out of shape." Living with change is unsettling, but it is tolerable so long as we remember that the Good News of Christ Jesus, and our duty to give glory to God through the power of the Holy Spirit, do not change. ✠

A Long Slow Process

Fellows Conference, College of Preachers,
Washington, D.C., April 1996

In Indianapolis in 1994, we struggled valiantly to effect more wide-ranging structural reform, but the Convention was not quite ready to make up its mind. So in this triennium we asked the Structure Commission to carry the study process forward, hoping to move closer to a consensus for the 1997 Convention in Philadelphia. The 1994 Convention specifically directed the Structure Commission to identify areas of overlap between and among the Interim Bodies, and we asked them to do this in the context of an overarching question: "if we had no structure, how might we best organize ourselves for the Church's mission?"

We do, of course, have an existing structure, and parts of it continue to function very well. Others are ready for modification, combination or even elimination—a process which has been going on continuously ever since we first adopted our Constitution in 1789.

Over the past several years, many groups and individuals have expended enormous amounts of love and energy and ideas and commitments and enthusiasm on the challenges of "re-structuring" the Episcopal Church. Some feel frustrated that there have not been any major changes in the Convention or Interim Body framework yet; but I think it's best not to rush to "solve the problems" until we have given time for God to transform our offerings and give us a common vision of who we are called to be for Christ in our time and place. From "who we are" will come the "how" of organizing ourselves. Form will follow function, structure will follow mission. ✠

MODELS FOR "RESTRUCTURING"

Fellows Conference, College of Preachers,
Washington, D.C., April 1996

Some have expressed excitement about a proposal—a vision—being developed by the Standing Commission on World Mission, which calls for moving from a centralized "national" agency to a coordinating "network of networks" supporting regional and local ministries. As outlined so far, the proposal suggests that staffing for each ministry network and for the coordinating "network of networks" would be supported through contributions from the program budget of the General Convention and from the participating network members, and that authority would likewise be shared among the constituent groups.

This proposal reflects the facts that communication technologies offer unprecedented opportunities for immediate sharing of information, and for wide participation in planning and implementing a wide range of activities; and contemporary organizational theory favors collaboration and consensus over hierarchical decision-making structures.

THE HAZARDS OF GENERALIZING

On first reading, the proposal has a good anti-authoritarian ring to it, and raises up an appealing image of widespread cooperation and participation. But in its present form I'm not sure it's quite as radically wonderful as some people want it to be, for several reasons: I think the Commission may be generalizing from the situation affecting world mission in a way that is not really appropriate to other mission areas. Until recently there was considerable conflict and competition among various Episcopal groups sponsoring volunteers and paid missionaries in different parts of the world. Fortunately, leaders in these ministries recognized that this was both counterproductive from an efficiency standpoint and, more importantly, presented a poor witness to the unifying love of Christ for all the world.

Several years ago, the Global Episcopal Mission Network—GEM—was formed as a neutral gathering where different missionary philosophies could be respected and common concerns worked through. This network—galvanized into unified action by the threat to funding for appointed missionaries in the General Convention Program budget in 1994—has proven beneficial in coordinating work and creating possibilities for cooperation among those with philosophical and theological differences. As a correction to the situation affecting world mission, there is no doubt that the "network" approach was something new and very beneficial.

It may not follow, however, that this model needs to be introduced into other areas of ministry which are part of the General Convention Program budget. Programs for ministry development, evangelism, stewardship, youth ministry, and so on, already function for the most part as coordinated networks supporting regional and local programs. They are neither independent, as was the appointed missionary program, nor centralized enterprises in the top-down hierarchical model we have come to distrust. Church Center staff working in these areas are successful only insofar as they cultivate and maintain widespread networks of provincial and diocesan contacts, from whom come suggestions for needed resources and training programs, and for whom the national staff people provide clearinghouse functions and coordinated planning for diocesan, provincial and national evangelism and stewardship conferences, youth events, anti-racism training, and countless other ministry support activities.

NETWORK OF NETWORKS

In programmatic terms, I believe, the "network of networks" model is already in place in many areas of the church's mission and ministry. The Commission's proposal also suggests that the financial support for this model should come from both the General Convention Program budget and from voluntary contributions from the various participating groups and from dioceses who choose to support particular ministries. In its present form, it is difficult to assess this financial component; but I confess to some skepticism about how it would work.

Our constitution and canons place the responsibility and authority for Episcopal Church program expenditures in the hands of the General Convention—a broadly-representative body which, cumbersome as it may sometimes seem, has over time proved to be an effective mechanism for discerning God's will for the Church. It's one thing to develop a voluntary coalition of independent groups, diocesan advocates and national staff to identify needs and develop programs, but I have a hard time picturing how such programs, or staff, would be supported if funds had to be sought annually from many different sources. And I am uneasy about the loss of accountability to the General Convention that would follow.

I look forward to seeing the next phase of the

Commission's developing model, and to how the Structure Commission may choose to incorporate World Mission's suggestions into their recommendations. It is all a part of the emerging "vision" for our ministries and their supporting organizational structures in the 21st century. ☩

LEGISLATIVE VS. EXECUTIVE POWERS— A CAUTION

Executive Council, Charleston, West Virginia, June 11, 1996

I want to register a caution as the interim bodies— including Executive Council—prepare recommendations and resolutions for the next Convention. We need to be careful not to confuse the legislative with the executive aspects of our organization.

Only the General Convention can legislate for the whole church. Only its officers can govern us, and only within the bounds set by the Convention. The Trial Court in the case of Bishop Righter made very clear that neither a court, nor the House of Bishops or Deputies acting separately, nor any group of individual bishops, clergy or laity, nor any staff unit, and certainly no single individual—has authority to impose a decision on the rest of us.

We think of ourselves as a hierarchical institution, and I suppose liturgically we are. But our polity protects us from rules and decisions handed down from "above." We rely instead on democratic legislative processes for decision-making, and parliamentary procedure that encourages the contribution of all points of view to the discussion. We also take our time about it, meeting for decision-making only once every three years, and requiring two consecutive votes on many topics. Between Conventions, Standing Commissions and Committees created by the Convention study emerging issues and prepare recommendations for the next legislative gathering.

That's the legislative aspect of our organizational life.

Complementing it is an administrative structure through which officers and staff, dioceses, agencies and individual Episcopalians implement the decisions made by the Convention. Some involve governance, such as creating new dioceses and consecrating bishops, certifying the prayer book and updating the canons. Others involve the mission of the church: supporting missionaries, investing funds responsibly and communicating church policy to civic authorities, maintaining networks for youth ministry and evangelism, theological education and stewardship.

The Executive Council stands at the intersection, responsible for overseeing implementation of the Convention's decisions about both governance and mission, and for monitoring the policy studies of interim bodies. It is a complex arrangement requiring continual adjustment; but its evolution over the 75 years since the Council was created has served us pretty well.

GOVERNANCE/ADMINISTRATION TEST: POLICY OR PROGRAM?

However, you've probably noticed that I've left out a few things. Our national structures do not divide neatly into policy and program units. Again and again the line between recommending policy and implementing program has proven elusive. Again and again we have set up entities to handle both policy and program in specific areas on behalf of the whole church: the Church Pension Group, Forward Movement Publications, General Board of Examining Chaplains, Council for the Development of Ministry, Board for Theological Education, and many others. We recently invented yet another hybrid policy/program category, "committees reporting to the Presiding Bishop and Council" such as Racism, now subsumed under JPIC (Justice, Peace and the Integrity of Creation) and the Status of Women.

Some of these are canonical and others exist simply by virtue of Convention resolutions. Some, like the Pension Group and Forward Movement, operate as fully independent agencies. Some function more as staff-assisted networks—the Council for the Development of Ministry and the BTE, for example. Some are fully in the hands of the volunteers appointed to serve on them, like most Standing Commissions and Committees, while others have become staff-directed programs with volunteer advisory boards. ☩

JUSTICE: FROM POLICY & PROGRAM TO MINISTRY

Justice Summit, Cincinnati, Ohio, February 27, 1997

Let me talk a little about the ever-evolving structure of the church, to set this Summit in context. The Executive Council serves as the interim governing body of the Episcopal Church between our General Conventions. In February of 1995, the Council created the body we now know as the Justice, Peace and Integrity of Creation committee—JPIC. JPIC is an "official" part of the Episcopal Church, and reports directly to the Council, which in turn reports to the General Convention. It is JPIC which called this Summit together.

The idea behind the Council's creation of JPIC was to provide a structure for the many different but related concerns of peace and justice. JPIC is based on a model of the World Council of Churches program, knitting together global peace issues, anti-racism, economic justice and stewardship of the environment.

The Executive Council gathered together all these ministries into the JPIC program, alongside the Jubilee ministries. Each element has been mandated by previous General Conventions. The planning for the Summit involved people active in the ecumenical, young adult, ethnic and women's ministries of our church—a model of inclusivity in action. These various ministries are inter-related aspects of the Church's response to the needs of the world. ☩

HOW COUNCIL HAS EVOLVED

Report and Proposal from Council to Convention, 1997

Executive Council carries out General Convention policies, oversees funds, and is accountable for implementation of programs authorized by Convention. These programs include the placement of appointed missionaries and volunteers for mission; coordinating refugee resettlement; providing financial and advisory support for mission partners in dioceses, domestic and overseas provinces; creating and distributing worship and educational resources; developing and maintaining networks of support for children and youth ministries, evangelism and stewardship, small church and ethnic ministry, clergy and lay professional training and deployment; ecumenical relations; and a myriad of related functions that enhance the church's witness at local, diocesan, national and international levels.

Our church has a loose, even eccentric structure. Its anomalies sometimes cause confusion and frustration, but overall it adapts well to changing circumstances with only an occasional need for major reform. The biggest of these reforms was the 1919 creation of the Executive Council (originally called the "National Council" until the 1952 creation of the National Council of the Churches of Christ created too much confusion).

The Presiding Bishop was titular head of the Council so long as he continued to serve as a diocesan bishop. Since 1944, the Presiding Bishop has been a full-time Primate, with overall administrative responsibility for the program staff. With this change, the Council's role gradually shifted away from hands-on (if intermittent) managerial oversight, to concentrate on a series of urgent social issues about which the Church was called to witness:

- civil rights and urban crises in the 1950s and 1960s

- peace issues, social responsibility in investments, and women's "place" in the 1970s and 1980s

- racism and sexuality in the 1990's

Only the General Convention can set ECUSA policy in these areas, but the Council must interpret that policy during the triennium, respond to new developments, and oversee program staff who implement the policies and provide support for ministries around the country and the world. ✠

COUNCIL'S CORPORATE MEMORY
Executive Council, New York City, November 6, 1997

Some of you may not know that I am actually beginning my seventh triennium on Executive Council! I was an elected member for six years beginning in 1979, and when I became Vice President of the House of Deputies in 1985, Bishop Browning as the new Presiding Bishop invited me to continue. In 1991 I assumed the President's chair in the House of Deputies and thus became Vice-Chair of this body.

So if anyone should know whether "we've always done it this way," it's me—and I'm here to tell you that part of the Council's strength has always been its flexibility and willingness to adapt to the realities of leadership in an ever-changing Church. ✠

WHAT GENERAL CONVENTION CAN DO
Episcopal Church Club, Philadelphia, September 21, 1999

There are only two ways the General Convention can speak "definitively"—by changing the canons or constitution, or by changing the authorized text of our worship, the Book of Common Prayer.

Changes to the Constitution or the Prayer Book must be adopted by two-thirds of the bishops and deputies at two successive conventions, and the vote in the House of Deputies must be "by orders": that is, two thirds of the diocesan lay deputations and two thirds of the diocesan clerical deputations must agree. That's a deliberately conservative method of voting, intended to prevent us from making major changes in our foundational documents without due consideration.

Changing the canons, or the supplementary worship materials that may be used if approved by the diocesan bishop, can be done by a single General Convention.

All other resolutions are simply advisory, expressions of the mind of that convention, indicating where the majority of bishops and deputies were on that question at that particular time.

THE LEGISLATIVE PROCESS

Resolutions are assigned to legislative committees, which will hold hearings, and may invite broad participation during several evening open dialogue sessions.

The committees will then bring the resolutions to one House, with a recommendation, which may be to adopt as is, to adopt with amendment, to adopt a substitute on the same topic, or to reject.

After debate in the House, a vote is taken. If it passes in one House, it goes to the other. If defeated by either House, it goes nowhere. If it passes in both, it becomes an "act of Convention."

Once you understand the basic framework, very similar to that of the US Congress, you see that the church's legislative process is pretty straightforward, at the General Convention as well as in your diocesan convention.

Many steps are involved, which insures that many voices are heard at each stage. Right up to the moment of voting, parliamentary procedure protects the right of everyone to be heard. It's a system which assumes there will be disagreements, and even serious conflict, but calls on everyone to stay within the agreed-upon process whether their resolution is adopted this time or not.

The vast majority of the House of Deputies at the last two conventions clearly had confidence in the process, and were willing to live with ambiguity when the legislative process did not produce a clear result. I have every expectation that the Deputies will behave similarly in Denver. This doesn't mean that everybody was or will be happy. That's not possible, when we hold such sharply divergent views. But God will be with us in our divisions as well as our unity. ✠

Conflict Is Normal

Diocese of Western Michigan Convention, October 8-9, 1999

I firmly believe that God will be with us in our divisions as well as in our unity, when we faithfully enter "hospitable conversation," and when we fail.

Our ancestors had an unfortunate habit of terminating those with whom they disagreed. Lest we feel too superior, I'm sure that centuries from now, our descendants will point to equally unfortunate habits which to us seem standard operating procedure. But things have improved. We learn, we change, we grow.

Whether we look backwards, or peer into the future, it's evident that conflict and its eventual resolution are a normal part of the life of the church. It's true throughout Christian history. It's true of the Episcopal Church. There's not a diocese in this church that hasn't had its share of fights over churchmanship or money, competition among congregations, scandal, conflict over buildings versus mission—you can make your own list. Through it all, the People of God continue, through the grace of God. ✠

CONVENTION'S AUTHORITY AND LIMITS

March 2000 Column in Episcopal Life

General Convention has the authority to change the documents that define us as Episcopalians: the constitution and canons and the Book of Common Prayer, along with its accompanying Hymnal and supplemental music and worship texts.

It must also authorize use of national resources and staff who coordinate various missionary, educational and social-justice ministries, and adopt a budget to support them.

These are General Convention's chief canonical responsibilities. Historically, the convention has also considered resolutions addressing a broad range of ecclesiastical and social policy issues.

Some policies, if they are written into our constitution and canons, or are implicit in authorized worship materials, have the force of ecclesiastical law. As such, they are binding on all Episcopalians, and especially on the clergy, whose ordination vows include a promise of obedience to them.

Other policy statements are expressions of the mind of the majority of deputies and bishops at a particular convention. They shape the agenda for the public policy work of the church and serve as guidance on issues for dioceses, congregations and individual Episcopalians, but they are advisory rather than mandatory.

WHAT RESOLUTIONS ARE NOT

This distinction has been much debated over the years. A committee to study the matter more than a century ago, in 1877, recommended that convention vote only on canonical issues so as to be clear about what was authoritative. Other resolutions "have never been deemed to have, and ought not to be construed as having, the force of law but merely the expression of an opinion...of great weight indeed but not obligatory."

The "canon only" recommendation was defeated, and the puzzle continued. A report to the 1880 convention noted that any resolutions about the "force" of resolutions would themselves be resolutions, "neither more nor less, and...it is difficult to see how any real relief could come to embarrassed minds from our passing them."

I don't suspect we will find "relief for embarrassed minds" on this question any time soon. But I'm not sorry about that. We have historically been very cautious about making "mandatory" decisions via changes to the canons or the prayer book, which encapsulate the core of our theological tradition and our polity. Changing them is serious business, and should be done only after extended conversation throughout the church points to a new consensus.

Policy statements, "mind of the house" resolutions and similar guidelines may promote such conversation and influence decisions in the interim, but they are never the last word. ✠

> *Only a few people have the interest or patience to wrestle with the details of church finances, local, diocesan or national - but money is especially important in periods of institutional change. Her unusually long service on the Executive Council gave President Chinnis an exceptional knowledge of the budget process, and of the connections between organizational change and financial structures.*

Structures and Resources: Managing the Church's Money

"INTERNAL" RESTRUCTURING

Executive Council, Providence, Rhode Island, February 15, 1995

The financial situation, changes in the funding formula, and the budget adopted by the last Convention have required a series of cuts and realignment of program activities at the Church Center. The surprise resignation of the Treasurer last month contributes further to that state of flux, and I want to assure you that Bishop Browning and I are working closely together throughout this process.

The relationships among the General Convention, the Council, and the staff have gone through many permutations in the 75 years since Canon 60 (as it was then numbered) established a "Presiding Bishop and Council" to "administer and carry on the Missionary, Educational and Social work of the Church." I venture to say those relationships will continue to evolve in response to changing circumstances. It is good to note here, for the record, that in the 1990's the Presiding Bishop, the "Presiding Deputy" and key members of the Executive Council and Joint Standing Committee on Program, Budget and Finance are collaborating closely with senior staff to maintain an appropriate balance of power among our various centers of institutional authority. ✠

CRISIS MUST NOT DIVERT US FROM MISSION

Executive Council, Seattle, Washington, June 13, 1995

Faithfulness to the past requires constant adaptation. It is in this context that I try to view the situation resulting from the management review last fall that led to the resignation of the Treasurer, the subsequent discovery of the embezzlement, and the sequence of legal, administrative and financial steps being taken in response.

Problems have been uncovered that need to be set right. Administrative functions need to be teased apart to restore balance with program responsibilities. Financial controls must be restored. Council must provide appropriate guidance and responsible oversight for staff who have—for years—been buffeted, demoralized, downsized, and often criticized "from the field" for carrying out the programs which Convention has authorized.

It is essential that we give attention to these financial and administrative matters; but let's not allow them to crowd out our primary commitment to the church's programs of mission, education and social service. Financial and administrative structures are only the means through which we exercise our ministry—to spread the Good News of Jesus Christ, to educate ourselves and our children in the faith which our ancestors passed on to us, to minister to the poor, the sick, the prisoners, the outcast.

As Council members we must attend with care to many administrative and financial details. However, we do not seek to be good stewards merely for the sake of being good stewards. We do it to make possible the mission of the Church by creating and adapting the institutional structures that support individuals and congregations in their ministries. ✠

TALKING ABOUT MONEY
Trinity Church, Staunton, Virginia, September 4, 1995

In my experience, Episcopalians find it difficult to talk frankly about money—at least in its personal dimension. We're usually adept at dealing with institutional funds (the embezzlement notwithstanding) whether in our business and professional life, or as members of the church vestry or diocesan budget committee, but we get pretty uncomfortable if the topic turns to how we allocate our own personal resources.

This discontinuity between public and private attitudes toward financial priorities and decision-making can have disastrous effects, because it creates a morally vulnerable spot, an entry-point for the powers of sin and darkness. This discontinuity contributed to our vulnerability to the embezzlement of so much money by the church's national treasurer, and I'd like to use that wretched situation as a cautionary tale to illustrate those hard words of Jesus: *None of you can become my disciple if you do not give up all your possessions.*

Using her insider's knowledge of the church's accounting system, and the authority of her own signature, the

Treasurer diverted 2.2 million dollars of church funds to her own personal use. With our money, she and her family enjoyed an opulent life-style: buying, remodeling, and furnishing two elegant homes, taking expensive vacations, riding to work each day in a chauffeured limousine, providing costly gifts and lavishly entertaining colleagues from the church center staff, and the clergy and lay people who served on various financial oversight committees for the national church. Although a few eyebrows were raised about this lifestyle of very conspicuous consumption, most of us assumed that the family was independently wealthy, and thus entitled to whatever lifestyle they chose.

CORPORATE AND PERSONAL ACCOUNTABILITY

If we had realized that it was church funds being used to support those personal extravagances, there would certainly have been a great hue and cry. But we thought it was her own money, and that it wouldn't be "polite" or appropriate to question how she chose to spend it. We were using different standards of accountability—of stewardship—for the church's resources than for the resources of individual church members: corporate resources should not be squandered, but spending personal wealth is a private matter.

It was this kind of thinking that made us vulnerable to an embezzlement of major proportions. Our stewardship of the church's funds was undermined because of an unvoiced assumption that the stewardship of personal funds is none of the community's business.

We are surrounded by consumer products, deluged by opportunities for recreation and entertainment— fine dining, art, music, theater, travel—and immersed in an atmosphere that suggests our worth as persons somehow depends on our possessions and our financial independence and power.

The Treasurer lost her way amidst these temptations, using our money. Are we not equally guilty of succumbing to a false value system, forgetting our accountability to each other for the use we make of the talents and treasures God has placed in our care?

THE HARD CHALLENGE OF STEWARDSHIP

Monks and nuns take this saying literally, renouncing personal ownership and witnessing to the value and freedom of a simple material life-style. Those of us not called to voluntary poverty as members of religious orders need to be aware of the moral danger of a strictly metaphorical interpretation of Christ's saying about possessions.

If we try to rationalize it away, we lose our moral bearings. If we ignore its challenge, we can't use our own resources faithfully, and we can't help others avoid the pitfalls of greed, deceit, theft and treachery. Where is the middle ground? Is there a middle ground of responsible Christian affluence? How will Christ judge my use of resources—and yours—as individuals, in our congregations, as the Episcopal Church in the USA?

The key to stewardship lies in accountability—recognizing that we are accountable to each other whether we want to be or not. How I spend my money does have an affect on you. The financial decisions of a congregation do affect the people in the surrounding community. Fifty or five hundred years from now people will look back and judge how well we used the resources at our disposal.

This is a hard saying if we trust in our own wisdom to set priorities, and to weigh needs and opportunities. But if we remember that we are only temporary caretakers entrusted with talents and treasure in order to build up the Realm of God, then we can count on God's grace and wisdom to keep us in the right path, to make our possessions blessings instead of curses, to help us choose life instead of death. ✠

IT'S MORE THAN JUST MONEY

Executive Council, Birmingham, Alabama, October 31, 1995

Sometimes it feels as though financial pressures are driving everybody's conversations about "structure"—the need to "downsize" and eliminate programs just because we can't afford to do everything we once did. But finances are a symptom, not a cause. They point to the depression and anxiety that cloud our perceptions of everything in these waning years of the 20th century, around the globe, and summon us to re-center ourselves in Christ, to recommit ourselves to our life together, in a disciplined community, guided not by our own human hopes and dreams but by a vision of God's love and purpose.

Archbishop Brian Davies of New Zealand has said "church leaders need to see themselves as vision bearers, not problem solvers." We must be vision bearers before we can do anything else. As leaders, as a Council, we must understand our first task as that of being open always to God's presence among us and to the discernment of God's will; and we can only do that if we suspend our own agendas and let the vision of God's agenda take shape in our hearts and minds. Then we can be problem solvers. Until then, we cannot even accurately recognize what the problems are.

There was a wonderful quotation from Archbishop Richard Holloway, Primus of Scotland, in the Anglican World magazine last Easter:

> *The large stone that closed the tomb where they laid the dead body of Jesus was easier to roll away than the tiny stones that effectively seal off our minds from the possibility of divine action. It's not sin or unbelief that keeps us entombed, it's lack of imagination. We just don't see how God can release us from our various graves...*

I deeply believe that if we can summon faith that it is

God's will to give new life to our institutional structures, our imaginations will be enlivened, and the tiny stones that seal us off from each other and weigh down our corporate efforts can be rolled away.

Something new is happening here. We are not doomed to our various graves forever. We have only to trust the Spirit, and give thanks that God calls us to love and service in our place and time. ✠

THE FINANCIAL STRUCTURE
Executive Council, Miami, Florida, February 9, 1996

One of the most important aspects of our structure is financial—where the money comes from and how decisions are made about spending it. Let me review where we presently stand—not in terms of the dollars we do or don't have, which I leave in the capable hands of our new Treasurer, but in terms of financial structures.

The canons provide for a two-part budget:

1. The **"General Convention Expense Budget"** includes the work of the interim bodies who prepare recommendations for Convention action; the expenses of the meeting itself—its planning, facilities, preparations, materials, and so forth; implementing Convention legislation by Executive Council and by the officers of the Convention, including the General Convention Executive Officer who coordinates the work of its Secretary and Treasurer, the Presiding Bishop, and the President of the House of Deputies (whose position is unsalaried, but travel expenses and office support are provided).

2. In addition to the Convention Expense Budget, the canons also provide for a **"Program Budget"** which covers the communications, resources and staff needed to carry out missionary and educational programs

authorized by the Convention. The Program Budget pays for the ministries which the church has decided are best done with centralized support. In some cases the Program Budget funds administration of a particular function on a national basis for everyone. For example: the Migration Ministries Program provides a one-stop place for dioceses and parishes to connect with the government in the placement and care of refugees; the Church Deployment Office is a clearinghouse for clergy and lay professionals throughout the church. More often, it is support services for local ministries, such as Children's Ministries and Stewardship, which are provided centrally—communications networks, training materials and conferences, educational resources.

The Program Budget pays for the ministries we have decided to do together as Episcopalians. The Convention Expense Budget pays for what makes us the Episcopal Church in the first place. The General Convention establishes our institutional existence as a group of dioceses bound together by: worship from a common prayer book; a common constitution and canons; the House of Bishops and the episcopacy, for which the Presiding Bishop is chief caretaker through his role in the consecration process; and the House of Deputies which secures the role of clergy and laity in our decision-making processes.

Until 1994, contributions from dioceses to support the national budget were in two parts: a mandatory "assessment" for the General Convention, the basic government of the church; and a voluntary "apportionment" supporting missionary and educational programs at home and abroad.

THE INDIANAPOLIS EXPERIMENT

Something new was tried in 1994. The former Treasurer and the Joint Standing Committee on Program, Budget and

Finance (PB&F) brought a recommendation to Executive Council, after consulting with diocesan financial officers. Their proposal, which Council endorsed, called for consolidating the Convention Expense and Program budgets, and combining the diocesan assessment and apportionment into a single asking. Recognizing the financial pressures facing the dioceses, the budget forwarded by Council cut back the Convention Budget, and stripped Program drastically.

When he addressed the Joint Session on the budget, Presiding Bishop Browning gave eloquent voice to the distress of many about curtailing the church's mission, and challenged Bishops and Deputies to a leap of faith. We adopted a two-tiered approach quite different from the two-part budget prescribed in the canons. The first level supports the stripped-down budget for both Convention Expenses and Program, funded by a single diocesan asking. The second "challenge" level was to restore cuts only if and when receipts of the voluntary askings exceed the initial bare-bones budget.

Bishops and Deputies pledged to return home and work to see their dioceses rise to the challenge. Some have done so, even sacrificially. But many others have found diocesan incomes lagging. As parishes fall behind in diocesan support—whether due to inflationary pressures and static giving, or an intentional redirection of support to local ministries—dioceses have less to pass along to the national budget.

The mandatory assessment for the Expense Budget was dropped in the consolidated budget, with the understanding that the so-called "canonical" expenditures for Convention would be protected in the event of shortfalls. But shortfalls have proven greater than anticipated, and for the first time ever the portion of the budget which supports the basics of our church's government is affected along with support for mission and ministry programs.

TIME TO RE-ASSESS—
MONEY AND DISCONTENT

I feel some concern about this, and am glad we decided to go ahead and experiment with the new approach before changing the canons. As we approach the budget process for the next triennium, I urge careful consideration of this matter. Although it seemed like a good idea at the time to many people, I'm not sure combining the Convention and Program Budgets, in effect making the entire diocesan contribution voluntary, has proven beneficial.

In every period of division and distress, some people express their discontent by withholding funds. Several times in the past, this has curtailed Church Center program activities supporting the ministries of dioceses and parishes. The survival of our basic decision-making structure was assured, however, through the mandatory assessment for the Convention Expense Budget.

That was a financial reflection of the unifying role which the episcopacy plays in the Episcopal Church. The bishops' spiritual authority comes through ordination in the Apostolic Succession, but their ecclesiastical authority derives from the General Convention.

There are some denominations which do not have this expression of unity. Their national structures are strictly voluntary, and when conflict arises local congregations can direct contributions to competing agencies. A few voices in our church want us to behave in the same way. Some even call for abolishing the General Convention altogether. I don't think those who voted for a consolidated budget in 1994 anticipated or intended that result.

I want us to continue to support our national decision-making structures. Their framework embraces our diverse community as we wrestle with serious conflict. Like the theological principle of the via media, our structure provides a shared space for debates about the direction God is calling us, and reminds us that the things which unite us are stronger than those which divide us.

Conflict is messy and often very painful, but we live in an age in which it cannot be avoided. Vexing questions about who may be ordained, or what kinds of relationships God requires, won't just go away. We must stick with them until God leads us to a resolution, and our basic Convention structure is a good one for this purpose.

The parliamentary process encourages listening to many voices in the process of corporate discernment. The conservative effect of requiring passage in two houses, and in both orders of the House of Deputies whenever people feel strongly about an issue, gives us mechanisms for NOT making important decisions before a critical level of consensus has been reached.

This approach to government has served us well since the time this church was established. It brought us through the wrenching changes from an agricultural to an industrial society. I believe it will prove particularly well suited to the shifting dynamics of the new information era, in which speed and broad access to information will dramatically increase autonomy at the local level. Let's not lose sight of the financial implications of maintaining the governance framework that enables us to work together. ✠

HOW WE PAY FOR PROGRAM
Executive Council, Charleston, West Virginia, June 11, 1996

Let me build on a spirited discussion with the Joint Standing Committee on Program, Budget and Finance (PB&F) about the "consolidated budget." You know that I have had misgivings about this approach because it risks confusing our governance and program functions. In addition, eliminating the Assessment and consolidating the Convention Budget and the Program Budget into a single Asking can appear to make diocesan financial support of our governing body and the Primate voluntary. I don't believe that's what we intend.

The canons presently require funding the General Convention Budget through mandatory assessments to every diocese, linking participation in our government with financial support for it. If we change the canons to authorize a consolidated budget, we must be very careful not to alter the fundamental nature of the covenant between the Episcopal Church in the USA and its constituent dioceses.

The consolidated budget is an approach to the question, how do we make sure we can pay for program? Bishop Browning has argued eloquently about the importance of program to the life of the Church. There are many aspects of our ministry and witness that benefit from the coordination and expertise possible when we pool resources for a common effort. But there can be no program without an authorized agency to carry it out, and there can be no agency without a strong General Convention to authorize it and provide financial resources.

NOT A NEW ISSUE

It is helpful to remember that this is an old, old debate. From the moment the Domestic and Foreign Missionary Society was established in 1820 it "competed" with dioceses for financial support of program. Some bishops refused to authorize chapters of the Society in their dioceses, fearing they would drain funds from local work. Others recognized the value of cooperative effort and supported "national" programs for missionary sending and religious education, but the tension remained.

A hundred years later, when Council was formed to administer consolidated programs for missionaries, religious education and social service under the umbrella of the Domestic and Foreign Missionary Society, opponents argued that "bureaucracy" would eat up funds needed for local ministry. When the Presiding Bishop's job became a full-time thing, the same argument was made. In the 1950's—which so many like to think of as the golden age of the American Church—a letter in *The Living Church* complained:

> *The Church is being taken out of the hands of its members, and being made the property of a small, clever, liberal clique who try to impose their partisan policies on everyone.**

Does this sound familiar? ✠

CONSOLIDATE BUDGET—REVISITED
Program, Budget & Finance, March 1997

Most of you will remember the sometimes-heated discussion last year when I questioned the wisdom of continuing the experiment with a consolidated budget. At that time I was resoundingly out-voted, and I don't expect many to be pleased that I am bringing up the subject again. But I am bringing it up again, and I ask you to bear with me as I try to set forth the reasons for my very deep concern.

My continuing objections to a single budget fall into two categories: the effect of this change on the fundamental polity of the Episcopal Church, and the practical consequences of making such a change at this particular moment in our history.

BUDGET & POLITY

How money is collected and spent establishes the basic character of any institution. The General Convention Expense Budget is established in Canon 1 of Title I. It is to cover the expenses of the General Convention itself, and of its two

---

*The Living Church, October 12, 1958, p. 16-17; as quoted in *The Role of the Presiding Bishop* by Roland Foster, Forward Movement, 1982, p. 101.

presiding officers, and it is to be raised by direct assessment levied upon each diocese.

The General Convention is the governmental structure of the Episcopal Church in the United States of America. According to our constitution, this church is "a Fellowship within the One, Holy, Catholic, and Apostolic Church, of those duly constituted Dioceses, Provinces, and regional Churches in communion with the See of Canterbury, upholding and propagating the historic Faith and Order as set forth in the Book of Common Prayer" [Preamble to the ECUSA Constitution].

This fellowship of dioceses is governed by the General Convention consisting of representatives from every member diocese organized into two houses, of bishops and of deputies. Our Constitution gives the Convention authority over our worship and theology as embodied in the Book of Common Prayer, our discipline as embodied in the canons, and our ministry and membership through the consent process for episcopal ordinations and the admission of dioceses to "union with the General Convention." These are the fundamental elements of our polity, and the General Convention Expense Budget supports that governmental structure.

INTRODUCTION OF THE PROGRAM BUDGET

What we know as "The Program Budget" did not come into existence until the reorganization of 1919 created a new canonical entity known as "the Presiding Bishop and Council." Before 1919, various church-wide "program" ministries were organized outside the constitutional structure of the church itself. They raised their own funds through voluntary subscription, and had independent boards responsible for directing staff and expending those funds.

The oldest of these is the Domestic and Foreign Missionary Society, first created in 1821 by a declaration of the General Convention that every member of the Church was also a member of the Society. Like many Convention resolutions, this one was only a little more valuable than the paper it was printed on. For almost a century, the Society struggled to carry out missionary activities at home and abroad. Its Board consisted of the bishops whose dioceses gave money to the Society.

There was also a Board of Religious Education, with a similar structure for supporting the Sunday School movement, providing curricular materials and training. By the end of the 19th century another church-wide program was developing, as Episcopalians took a lead in responding to issues of social justice. In this instance, funding was initially slipped into the General Convention budget through allocations for the Standing Commission on Social Service, but there was bitter opposition to this.

The reorganization in 1919 was the next logical step. The Presiding Bishop and Council were given responsibility for "the unification, development, and prosecution of the Missionary, Educational, and Social Work of the Church, and of such other work as may be committed to it by the General Convention" [Canon 1.4 (1)a].

Along with this responsibility came the authority to propose a "Program Budget" to fund these church-wide ministries. Unlike the Convention Expense Budget, which is supported by direct assessment levied on every diocese, the Program Budget was to be supported by an "apportionment." In other words, the Council replaced the independent boards of each program, Council members becoming ex officio the Board of the Domestic and Foreign Missionary Society, which was now responsible for religious education and social issues as well as missionary work.

Fund-raising for all programs was combined into a single request. This new canonical approach to supporting program expenses assumed direct support from congregations, channeled through the Diocese. The Executive Council informs each diocese of what its proportionate share of program costs will be, and the diocese is to tell each parish and mission how much it should raise to meet this objective.

STRUCTURE AND IDENTITY

I dwell on these details of canon and history because I think they tell us something very important about our identity as a national church. As an institution, we are still first and fundamentally a fellowship of dioceses bound constitutionally through the Prayer Book and the ordained ministry, regulated by the General Convention. That is the bottom line of our institutional commitment to each other.

Program is not government. Program is an expression of our identity as Anglicans in this country, but the shape and extent of program necessarily evolves in response to the world in which we minister.

The ministries that flow from our baptismal covenant—ministries of evangelism and education and response to human need and social injustices—are not "national" programs. They begin in the work and witness of individual Episcopalians—ordained and lay—in congregations and dioceses throughout the church. Over the years it has been helpful and economical to work together in certain areas: coordinating missionary deployment, providing education and training, and creating resources for particular ministries such as school and prison chaplaincies, fellowships of prayer and bible-study, and so forth.

Most of this cooperation has been done via independent agencies, from the DFMS in its 19th century form to the multitude of unofficial groups, agencies, organizations and associations which support Episcopalians in their ministries to this day. Some aspects of program have been brought under the umbrella of the General Convention through incorporation into the Program budget—when there was some consensus about how a particular ministry was to be conducted. But the Canons and the General Convention have heretofore always allowed congregations and dioceses to determine the extent to which they are going to support these cooperative ministry programs.

Bishops and Deputies adopt a program budget, and are supposed to return home and educate congregations and diocesan bodies about the importance of contributing to the church-wide ministries of evangelism, witness and service included in that budget. It is the local church, through its diocesan framework, that must ultimately decide how much to raise and how to spend it on program and ministries at home and abroad.

In short, paying for the government of the Episcopal Church has always been mandatory. Paying for the programs through which the church carries out its mission in particular times and places has always been voluntary, in the local congregation, at the diocesan level, and through programs authorized by the General Convention, as well as through all the unofficial, independent groups that support our spiritual, educational and justice ministries.

A consolidated budget supported by a single asking stirs government and program together in one pot and makes the entire thing voluntary. On a philosophical level, this dramatically undermines what has been our basic polity. There are grave practical consequences as well.

BUDGET AND UNITY IN AN AGE
LACKING CONSENSUS

When a diocese is accepted into unity with the General Convention, it accepts the Convention's authority over the prayer book, the constitutions and canons, and the financial assessments that support these basic structures. Once part of the Episcopal Church, no diocese is free to pick and choose parts of the prayer book or the legal structure, or the financial obligations of membership.

History shows that dioceses have been faithful in their efforts to meet their assessments, often despite great economic pressure at home, and through periods of profound conflict about theological issues or social policy. Even in the past triennium, dioceses most at odds with the General Convention have continued to calculate and pay that portion of their asking designated for the "canonical" section of the budget.

We've never had canonical penalties for refusing to pay the assessment for the General Convention Expense Budget, because everyone has always understood that—to put it crudely—we can't play if we don't pay, because there won't be any game. We accept the financial cost of being the Anglican presence in this country. We don't question whether to be the Episcopal Church.

History also shows that we generally use financial weapons in our battles over theology, ethics, politics and social issues. Support for the Program Budget has waxed and waned depending upon the degree of consensus about how the Episcopal Church and its elected leaders witness in the world. Dissatisfaction with the elected leadership of General Convention and Executive Council spills over into anger with the staff of the Episcopal Church Center who implement the Program Budget.

Withholding money for program becomes a way of saying, "we are unhappy with what's happening." It is also a way of reasserting the fact that we are a bottom-up fellowship of dioceses rather than a top-down centralized bureaucracy. You all know how much interest there is now in limiting bureaucracy and decentralizing responsibility for the program ministries of the Church. In this context, the pressure for a consolidated budget can be seen as a desperate bid by a beleaguered institution to hang onto its centralized power by restricting diocesan discretion over program initiatives.

It's a very weak bid, however, because instead of making program mandatory along with government, it would make both voluntary. The consequences are not hard to predict. Voluntary askings are notoriously unreliable. At least a third of the dioceses experimenting with voluntary systems in 1993 had restored mandatory assessments by 1996.

We are in a transition time, in which consensus on many important issues does not exist. That situation is not going to improve significantly in the next decade. Do we really want to set up financial incentives for rejecting the authority of the General Convention? PB&F's report to the General Convention itself states the principle that "when money runs out we are honored to keep only the covenant with the structure that makes us the Episcopal Church in the USA" (1997 Blue Book, p. 381). Why then do we propose canonical changes that weaken that very structure?

The Blue Book is being printed. The Proposed Program Budget has been adopted by Executive Council. The consolidated budget train is on track and headed for the finish line. I ask you not to let those circumstances prevent us from reconsidering now, before we get to Philadelphia.

If it's easier to administer expenditures through a consolidated accounting system, fine. But let's clearly divide the income side between that which sustains the governmental structures of the Church and that which supports program. Continue the former as a mandatory assessment and the latter as a voluntary asking, and administer the income in accordance with that distinction.

A VERY BAD PRECEDENT

That was the intention last time—to protect the "canonical" side of the budget against cuts if income fell below projections. But it didn't quite work out that way.

In the wake of the embezzlement, an interim Treasurer, a new Chief Operating Officer, the Executive Council, and PB&F were bent on regaining the control we had so clearly lost. With income down severely in 1995, staff proposed cuts in the General Convention budget along with the program budget. In the crisis of the moment, officers of the Convention—including myself—were persuaded to go along with these cuts. I believe we made a mistake, but the precedent was set, and has continued. We need to stop that now, instead of institutionalizing it by enshrining it in the canons.

I hope PB&F will decide at this meeting to withdraw the resolutions that amend the Joint Rules and the Canons to authorize a consolidated budget. In their place we would offer a substitute resolution similar to the one used in 1994, to permit further experimentation with a new approach to budget management. This would give us all another triennium to consider the ramifications, and give the new financial team time to develop its own approach instead of being locked into something developed during the former Treasurer's tenure.

We would also need to be prepared with a re-organized set of figures for Philadelphia. This could use a single percentage-of-diocesan-income formula if desired. But we would identify the appropriate portion of that total as a mandatory assessment to support the basic structure of the Church.

I strongly believe that such an important change in the nature of this church must be widely debated by the General Convention. Discussion should not be short-circuited by presentation of a budget document that, in effect, requires canonical changes which would fundamentally affect our polity. ✠

REITERATING THE ALARM

Union of Black Episcopalians, Hampton, Virginia, June 24, 1997

An issue facing Convention this summer, dealing with polity and accountability, is the reappearance of a "unified budget" which was adopted without canonical justification at the last Convention. This time, the Program, Budget and Finance Committee is proposing canonical changes to justify continuing the unified budget, which in my view makes our basic governing structures needlessly and dangerously vulnerable to whimsical fluctuations in diocesan support for the church's budget. ✠

Despite these cautions, the 1997 General Convention did adopt canonical changes creating a consolidated budget. That battle lost, President Chinnis turned her attention to implementation, including the apportionment of funds to the "interim bodies," the commissions, committees, boards and agencies which function between General Conventions, previously included in the General Convention Expense Budget.

THE BUDGET VIS-À-VIS THE SO-CALLED "INTERIM BODIES"

Program, Budget & Finance, September 15, 1998

The Standing Commission on Structure's report to the 1997 Convention highlighted the concern that committees had multiplied and some "policy-making" bodies were too involved with program activities. However, Structure's recommendations to reduce the number of "interim bodies" actually resulted in an affirmation of the work of most of these groups. There was no wholesale elimination of committees and commissions. Rather, there was a review of how these groups serve the Church, and a redefinition (for many) of their canonical mandates. However, it was not possible for either PB&F or the staff to project accurately how much money would be needed by these reconfigured groups during this triennium.

Efforts to improve stewardship of support for the "Interim Bodies" led to the same Convention's approval of PB&F's "block grant" process (under which groups were to apply for funds for their work), but during the following year, it became clear that this approach hinders implementation of the mandates given to the committees, commissions, boards and agencies of the General Convention.

WHO DECIDES?

The process undertaken by Executive Council since the Minneapolis Convocation of "interim bodies" in early 1998, allocating funds directly to each of them in response to their requests, sought to balance the concerns of all the committees, commissions, boards and agencies of the General Convention. While the outcome did not satisfy all, given fiscal limitations based on income projections, it was a remarkable effort. However, questions have been raised as to whether the necessary adjustments shouldn't have been handled by the officers of Convention, rather than the chairs of the Standing Committees of Council. During the vacancy in the position of Executive Officer and Secretary of Convention, the Executive Committee of Program, Budget & Finance, a joint standing committee of the Convention itself, should have been consulted when financial support of groups created by and reporting to General Convention was in question. I'm sure this was the result of inadvertent carelessness, but it was another bad precedent.

Should the funding allocated to these canonical groups not enable them to complete their Convention-mandated work during the triennium, then PB&F and Council will need to act further, and to report on developments to the next General Convention. ✠

ORGANIZING THE SO-CALLED "UNIFIED" BUDGET

Executive Council, Oklahoma City, Oklahoma, November 3, 1998

In mid-September I met with the Joint Standing Committee on Program, Budget and Finance. One important focus of our work at that meeting grew from the discussions about budget that surrounded the decision to cancel the 1999 Convocation of Interim Bodies. I'm not going to go into the labyrinthine decision-making process that led to the cancellation. I will say that one of the silver linings has been clarification of some distinctions that were in danger of being lost.

Let me summarize the key points I made to PB&F:

- First, the "unified" budget requires us to respect the funding priorities in the "canonical" section of the budget. The officers of the General Convention are responsible for any necessary reallocation of funding for the committees, commissions, boards and agencies of the Convention.

- Second, we need to remember the differences among groups that serve the Convention. Let's reduce our use of the catchall term "Interim Body" to describe these entities, which actually differ significantly from one another. This will help us assign support for these groups to appropriate areas of the budget, as follows:

- **Standing Commissions and Joint Standing Committees** are primarily "policy-recommending" entities, identified by their canonical mandates and descriptions in the Canons and Rules of Order. While some are also related to the delivery of program services, the eleven Standing Commission budgets are clearly part of the canonical section of the budget.

- The **Executive Council** is itself a canonical entity with policy responsibilities. The expenses of the Council and its Standing Committees are properly located in the canonical portion of the budget.

- On the other hand, **Committees and Commissions of Executive Council,** created by Convention Resolution (i.e., not by canon), are responsible for both policy recommendations and program support for the special concerns and networks they represent. These groups report and are accountable to Executive Council. Their funding could fall within the portion of the budget that supports the work of the associated program unit at the Church Center. JPIC (Justice, Peace and Integrity of Creation) already presents us with a model, as their support comes solely from the related Program area of the budget. Similarly, other groups—Status of Women, HIV/AIDS Commission, Sexual Exploitation, and the newly formed working group on Science, Technology and Faith—might all be included in related Program areas of the budget, instead of within the block grant for Standing Commissions.

- **Boards and Agencies,** including those within the General Convention budget process (Archives,

Church Deployment Board and the General Board of Examining Chaplains) and those outside that process (Church Pension Fund, Forward Movement and General Theological Seminary) should continue to be represented and handled as separate budget entities.

Finally, although "Standing Commissions" are policy-recommending groups, some also have canonical program responsibilities and counterparts within the program portion of the budget. The budgets for such Church Center offices as Liturgy and Music, Stewardship, Ecumenical Relations, World Mission, and Professional Ministry Development should be structured and funded to respond to the program mandates given to their associated Standing Commissions by each Convention. These offices would then account to General Convention for these program components, through the Blue Book reports of the Standing Commissions.

All these recommendations would facilitate proper allocation of our resources in support of the acts of General Convention. They will also help us be clearer about the important distinction between program, which implements decisions already made by General Convention, and policy recommendations which await General Convention authorization. ✠

> *President Chinnis reads widely, in both the church and the secular press, and has the ability to make connections between seemingly disparate ideas and events. She developed an acute sense of the way changes in the world around it were affecting the church, and of the need for flexibility in responding to these changes.*

The Church in a Changing World

OF STEWARDSHIP AND CHALLENGES
Executive Council, New York City, October 31, 1994

In our household of faith the best description of the Executive Council's relationship to the General Convention is a metaphor from Scripture: Council is to act as the faithful steward of the vineyard of General Convention. Like the steward, we labor on behalf of others, and are accountable to others.

In the last triennium, Council had to respond to many conflicting realities as it exercised this stewardship, and we will encounter many of these same conflicts again. We are increasingly aware that existing patterns of institutional church life do not serve us adequately, yet we are also aware that change is a risky and anxiety-laden process.

Persuaded that sharing the Good News of Jesus Christ requires speaking in terms comprehensible to those around us, we must struggle to learn what that means when a consensus of culture, values and meaning does not exist. Committed to the centrality of vital lay ministry in the Church's mission, we must discover its implications for our institutional structures—which developed over many centuries during which the ordained were expected to provide all leadership and ministry to and for the laity.

These vital concerns are constantly in danger of being overshadowed by the acute and unpredictable financial pressures we experience as a church and society caught in an increasingly volatile world economy. Being good stewards will be a challenge for us! ✠

BLESSED ARE THE POOR

All Saints Church, Las Vegas, Nevada, February 12, 1995

Although it is an institution, the Church has many person-like attributes. People need some kind of income to live, to provide food and clothing and housing for physical survival, and to pay for communication, education and recreation to stay emotionally and spiritually healthy. The institutional church, too, needs income, to provide the physical equipment and buildings for its worship and mission programs, and to pay for education, spiritual formation, salaries to support the people who carry out those programs. All these things are necessary to the proper functioning of the human body, and the Body of Christ.

But Jesus says blessed are the poor and hungry. I don't think he was trying to glamorize poverty. There are plenty of other passages in which he makes it clear that we are called to help alleviate the suffering of those who are poor. But this assertion that the poor—not just the poor in spirit, but the really poor—are blessed needs to be taken seriously. They are blessed, he says, because the kingdom of God is theirs. Not "will be" but IS here and now. ✠

SCRIBES AND PHARISEES

When we have plenty, or at least enough, when our tummies are full and we feel fine and everyone else thinks we're fine, then "Woe" to us, scribes and Pharisees—because we'll easily forget that without God nothing would be possible. Then it's easy to think we did it all ourselves, and to forget our need for God, and to lose sight of the astonishing Good News about the kingdom of God.

When our budget is balanced and the pews are packed and all the "right people" in town—or in Congress—are Episcopalians, and our meetings go smoothly and we're widely admired, then "Woe" to us—because we won't want to be told that the poor and the hungry and the persecuted are already in the Kingdom we think we're busy creating.

Neediness, poverty, or persecution can force us to recognize our utter dependence on God, and this can be as important for the institutional church as for individual men and women trying to work out their own salvation. I am often dismayed by the financial crises and the sometimes humiliating public disagreements and the violent conflicts surrounding —and even within—our beloved Church. Yet Jesus says that in our very poverty the Kingdom of God is ours, and that when we are ridiculed we should leap for joy, and that all our tears shall be turned to laughter. ✠

AN EVER-CHANGING CONTEXT

Executive Council, Providence, Rhode Island, February 15, 1995

There is an inescapable framework within which all our work must be done: our existence as a church within a society and world subjected to ever-increasing stresses and ever-accelerating change. There are days when I long for what I like to remember as the certainties and security of the past, and especially those flush and optimistic days of the 1950s and early '60s when church-going was the norm and our hopes were high.

But God has called us to lead this church through a different time, into a new millennium whose character we can only dimly imagine. We proceed in faith without knowing our destination. I thank God for calling me to accompany you on that journey. ✠

"DISCONTINUITY" OF PERCEPTION AND REALITY

Executive Council, Bellevue, Washington, June 13, 1995

I have been struck by the amazing variety of local ministry happening around our church, and by the fact that much is supported—directly and indirectly—by the human and material resources authorized by the General Convention and provided by Church Center staff. In many cases, however, the local beneficiaries simply do not realize that connection. There is a discontinuity between their perceptions of the church beyond their own locality and the reality of their connections with it.

Somehow, many people seem to have put "the national church" into a separate category in their minds, unrelated to the use they make of the services of the Youth Ministry Office or the Evangelism network, the broad array of congregational development and stewardship materials, training for children's ministry, lay leadership, clergy deployment, grants for refugee resettlement or economic justice, liturgical materials and bible study guides, resources on everything from AIDS to a map of the church in Zaire, from models for small churches to violence against women.

The services available to the whole church from the

existing network of volunteers and diocesan, provincial and national staff are amazing in their breadth and value. We don't have to invent a lot of new things so much as we need to spread the word so more local ministries can take advantage of them. We need to turn around the rhetoric that perceives decisions and programs being handed down from on high, imposed by the "national church" on hapless congregations.

Let us do this in a spirit of trust and faith, resisting the pressures to careen from crisis to crisis without thought of our larger duty. The Episcopal Church has been around for a couple of centuries; the followers of Jesus Christ have been organizing themselves for evangelism and service for almost two millennia. The shape of this church for the next few years is in our hands, but the life of the Body of Christ, past, present and to come, is safely in the hands of God. With that assurance, we can keep present crises in perspective, tend efficiently to the administrative and financial necessities, and reserve our best energies for the mission and ministry of the Church. ✠

THE CHANGING CONTEXT OF MINISTRY

Episcopal Church Women, Diocese of Connecticut, May 2, 1996

Part of preparing ourselves for the next millennium—in the Church as well as in the world around us—is to look with a critical eye at the way things have been, the way they are, and the way we want them to be.

It's hardly news that everything in the external world is changing at an ever-increasing rate. Our grandmothers would be astounded by the tools we have for doing our work today—from microwave ovens and multi-cycle washer/ dryers to portable phones and fax machines and laptop computers. Kids can take the encyclopedia to the local copy shop for a color reproduction of a picture of a volcano to illustrate a report for science class. Grandparents in California can exchange e-mail messages with their granddaughter in Yale's freshman class. We can do all our Christmas shopping without ever leaving the easy chair by the telephone. Women operate fork lifts and practice medicine and argue before the Supreme Court and run companies and celebrate the Eucharist and fly on the space shuttle, in addition to having babies and raising children.

American society has evolved from an agricultural economy to an industrial society, and from there to a high-tech world of instant communications and global financial markets. A mushrooming world population is rapidly pushing the limits of space and resources to maintain life on this planet. The changes we have to deal with in our generation are as extraordinary as those which faced our ancestors who settled the American colonies, or followed wagon trains to the west, or left the farms of the dustbowl for the factories of the cities.

Fortunately, the God we worship and the Good News of the Gospel are the same yesterday, today and forever. But the Church's organization has had to adapt itself from one era to the next. We are in the midst of another cycle of this organizational renewal just now, and it is disorienting and a bit frightening as well as exciting and full of promise. ✠

A POOR RESPONSE TO CHANGE

"One Body, One Spirit, One Hope"—On to Philadelphia
Province III Convocation, Hagerstown, Maryland, July 1, 1996,

Labels like "liberal" or "conservative," "traditionalist" or "progressive," are at best simplistic and misleading. The fact that we continue to use such labels reflects our awareness that there are radical differences within our ranks. As long as we are Anglicans, this will be the case. We are not called to an enforced unanimity that would make labels useless, but to a love that resists using labels as weapons, and a generosity of spirit willing to tolerate ambiguity and conflict no matter how painful it gets. It is getting very painful.

The limits of our willingness to endure ambiguity and conflict are being sorely tested. This is not, in itself, a bad thing. The whole world is being sorely tested, as ethnic, economic, religious and political conflicts proliferate around the globe. The church cannot escape pressure in this era of instant communication and multi-national everything. Instead we must respond with the resources of our faith: a dogged love for each other, an unwavering hope in the promises of Christ, and an absolute conviction that God wills the reconciliation of all. With God's grace we can use these resources to offer the world a model for promoting justice while maintaining unity and peace. ✠

A Time of Potential Risk

Executive Council, Toronto, Ontario, November 9,1996
Joint Meeting with Anglican Church of Canada

We are surrounded by opportunities to stretch beyond both national and denominational borders. At the same time, we are experiencing great turmoil within our structures. This is a time of tremendous potential, and it is also a time of great risk. Many say this period in the church's life is a time of change, realignment and redefinition as profound as that of the Reformation.

Such a comparison may or may not be helpful, but it does highlight the care with which we need to exercise our stewardship as leaders of the institutional church. What kind of a community are we—as Episcopalians, as Anglicans, as Christians in an increasingly secular culture? What kind of community should we be? What can we learn from the personal, small-scale experiences of community we share here to guide our decisions about large-scale issues of partnership, cooperation and commitment? How shall we minimize the risk of losing something essential as we renew and reform the structures that support our faith community?

RENEWING AND REFORMING COMMUNITY

There is a very mixed bag of factors and motivations contributing to our present openness to new relationships. In our lifetimes, we have seen the steady growth of an inter-dependent consciousness and of cooperative structures that have transformed the Anglican Communion through a series of quite deliberate developments:

- Stephen Bayne's appointment as first Executive Officer of the Communion, in 1960;

- the powerful effect of the MRI principles— Mutual Responsibility and Interdependence in the Body of Christ—promulgated at the Anglican Congress right here in Toronto in 1963;

- the creation of the Anglican Consultative Council, which first gathered in 1971, in Limuru, Kenya, and has just concluded its tenth meeting, in Panama;

- the 1981 establishment of the Inter-Anglican Theological and Doctrinal Commission, and the Eames Commission charged in 1988 with offering guidelines for maintaining unity as provinces ordain women to the episcopate;

- the never-ending Anglican Cycle of Prayer for and with each other around the clock and around the globe;

- the evolution of print and electronic communication networks among the provinces—so that today Anglicans in Nebraska or New Zealand or Nova Scotia can read intercession requests and press releases from the Archbishop's office in

Capetown or Canterbury minutes after they are issued.

All these tools and structures have nurtured the growth of those "bonds of affection" that unite Anglicans worldwide, even as the *BOOK OF COMMON PRAYER* multiplies and divides and adapts to local languages and cultures. From a motley collection of remnants of the Church of England in former British colonies, we have become an international commonwealth of believers more and more aware of our need for each other.

In this same period, a powerful ecumenical spirit has been at work, pruning and redirecting and bringing together various strands of Christianity to strengthen our witness in a religiously-pluralistic world culture. The suspicions, stereotypes and condemnations that lingered from the conflicts of the reformation are giving way to deepened awareness of the shame of our divisions and a resulting commitment to restore unity to Christ's Body, the Church.

ECONOMIC IMPETUS

There are less spiritual factors, too. We must admit that grinding economic forces drive us to give up our isolation and illusions of self-sufficiency. I would even go so far as to say that it has been the relentless financial squeeze of the last quarter-century that has finally got our attention, compelling us toward cooperation in mission and ministry. In the face of burgeoning needs—both physical and spiritual—throughout the world, the pressure of diminished resources requires that we give up some of our autonomy, our turf, our preferred "way we've always done it."

This is good, if it punctures our parochial pride and encourages mutual responsibility and accountability. It is not good if we turn to each other only out of desperation and fear, if we join together merely to pool our poverty. Rather we need to work very deliberately to share our faith and hope, to live out of the abundance of God's love, not the scarcity of our own declining coffers.

The steadily shifting balance of spiritual authority within the Anglican Communion—from the North Atlantic to the Global South, from the declining churches of the industrialized first world to the mushrooming congregations of the third world—is all a part of this reallocation of resources. Those of us who for so long could take for granted the availability of material resources are discovering how much we have let them substitute for spiritual riches within our common life. Who are the truly disadvantaged? ✠

CYCLES OF CHANGE

May 1997 Column in Episcopal Life

Change is intrinsic to life. Only inanimate things never change. We count on the cycles of day and night. Flowers burst forth in bloom, babies are born and grow. When change is predictable we handle it pretty well. In fact, it can be comforting when familiar seasons and activities roll around again.

Unpredictable change, on the other hand, is unsettling, even frightening. It takes energy to adapt. We may lose things we valued.

Every three years the Episcopal Church goes through a cycle of institutional change. We are now in that period of increased activity and anxiety leading up to the General Convention. The preparations create a sense of urgency and excitement, anticipation and dread.

From the Book of Acts untill today there has never been a time when conscientious Christians have not disagreed about matters of importance. However, our unity in Christ does not depend upon unanimity.

We have a governing structure and a legislative process explicitly designed to maintain institutional integrity while we struggle to discern God's will. We have disagreed heatedly over questions of missionary strategy, slavery, the use of candles or incense, civil rights, the role of women, the language of worship, and a thousand and one other matters.

Each conflict loomed immensely at the time, but in retrospect we see that some were more important than others. Remembering this can help us sit lightly in the midst of the present conflicts. God was with our fathers and mothers before us, and will be with our children too. So God will be with us as we wrestle with the questions of today. ✠

MILLENNIAL FAITH:
OUR PILGRIMAGE TO THE FUTURE

13th Annual Baiz Memorial Lecture, March 12, 1999
Calvary Episcopal Church, Pittsburgh, Pennsylvania

Now, as the ticking clock brings the 21st century inexorably toward us, there is an uneasy shifting of our identity in time. We have been 20th century people set over and against our 19th century forebears, with our "modern" identity defined in contrast to their "old" ways of doing things.

What happens next? Do we become 21st century people or will we be stuck, in the eyes of others, or in our own minds, back in the "old-fashioned" 20th century?

Ever since the 1990's began we have had a growing social and cultural awareness of nearing the end of the century. Magazines and newspapers and television have been full of "look back" features—the most important events of the 20th century, the most influential people, the inventions that changed our world, the worst disasters, the best photographs, the biggest movie hits, all that sort of thing.

It's partly nostalgia and media hype. But it also represents a genuine need to take stock of what has brought us to where we are, to revisit the things that have made us who we are, to be able to say, "I was there," or "I saw that," or maybe even, "no, that's not the way it was."

Corporate Remembering

This corporate remembering strengthens our personal and collective ties to the past, to our history, to our place in a scheme of things that we know stretches back much farther than 1900, back beyond the sepia photographs and Victorian bric a brac, beyond the Civil War and the War of 1812 and the American Revolution, before the tobacco plantations and the slave trade and the destruction of native peoples, before the Reformation and the Inquisition, the Dark Ages and barbarian invasions, the Crusades and the Roman Empire, all the blips on the world history timelines we may or may not have studied in school.

Looking back over our own history links us to the rest of our cultural history—not just the century or millennium now ending, but the ones before that, and before that, and before that until we are peering so far into the distant past that all we can see are myths and legends, shadows cast by fire at the mouth of the cave.

Among the shadows, we see Abraham and Sarah trusting God to seek a new home, Moses and Miriam leading the Israelites out of Egypt, Isaiah summarizing the nation's wisdom and pointing toward its fulfillment, Mary saying "yes" to an angel, Jesus of Nazareth, calling people like us to follow him, Jesus Christ, raised from the dead in glory.

Looking back over our history as a religious people we see people and events that form our Christian identity as surely as George Washington and the Civil War form our identity as Americans. Looking back over many centuries, before the establishment of the United States, or the Episcopal Church in the United States, reminds us that our identity is very complex, a weaving together of many different strands.

Things have not always been as they are now. Society has changed. The Church has changed. Our 19th or 15th or 5th century ancestors would no more recognize our worship services or our General Convention than they would our telephones and space shuttles.

Yet we know that what is now did flow from what was then. Beneath the disparate surface there is continuity, consistency, faithfulness to the original impulses and commitments that formed Christianity out of those ragtag disciples and spread the Gospel across the Western world.

As we reflect on such things while approaching a new millennium, it will be helpful to articulate the connections between us and our spiritual ancestors which define our identity as Christians. It will be good to strengthen, through remembering, the bonds which link us to the church of the New Testament, the Israelites in the wilderness, even as the chronological distance between us leaps into a new dimension.

FROM PAST TO FUTURE

But our millennial reflections must not end with looking backward, as known and comfortable as that might be. How will the identity formed in the past affect us in the unknown future? Here, I would suggest, there is a striking difference between a secular response to the question and a religious response.

In the secular realm, assumptions we have made about being 20th century people must all be redefined. Institutional patterns identified with 20th century developments will come under increasing scrutiny and pressure for change. The bright promises of science, technology, medicine, have dimmed as the mixed results of "progress" become more apparent. Science fiction nightmares become all too plausible. Neither technology nor democracy has freed the world from war, or hunger, or racism or cancer.

So I suspect that at least some of the institutional structures we now take for granted will morph into very different shapes in the years ahead. Some of that transformation will result from deliberate efforts to adapt and improve. Some of it will be propelled by forces we don't control, such as climate and changes within the earth itself, or the unpredictable effects of the World Wide Web on communications and commerce.

Although we can assume a certain consistency in our response to such changes, given what seem to be fundamental human characteristics, in fact our identity as secular citizens may become as dramatically different from today's as we are from the lords and serfs of a thousand years ago.

As people of faith, the externals of our common life—style of worship, congregational or diocesan organization, patterns of lay and ordained ministry, the language we use to express our faith—will certainly continue the same trajectory of development that has brought us from the epistles of Paul to the 1979 Book of Common Prayer.

But our baptismal identity should be affected not at all. Indeed, it is the constancy of the Christian community as bearer of the Good News, and the constancy of the Christian as redeemed child of God despite all our sins, that makes it possible for the institutional church to make its way through the wilderness that the future has always been.

I find it helpful to remember that our forebears at the beginning of the 19th century, or the 10th century, or the 3rd century, had no more idea about what the future would bring than we have about the 21st century. Yet, despite their ignorance, they were able to make a path through the wilderness of time, and to pass on down to us the central marks of humanity, and the bright shining doctrines of the Christian faith. This is our task as well. ✠

Being called to leadership in the Church is a vocation President Chinnis takes very seriously. God provides what is needed for the life of the Church, whether we can recognize that or not, and it is particularly important to remember that truth during periods of change and trial. 1995 was a terrible year of crisis and scandal in the Church. President Chinnis worked side-by-side with Presiding Bishop Browning in responding to these troubles, and drew from the experience some important conclusions for future leadership.

Leadership in a Changing Church

WHO ARE THE LEADERS?
National Network of Lay Professionals, Dallas, Texas, December 1, 1989

"We have this Ministry"...When we ask if the "church" has become sideline rather than mainline, we must remind ourselves that "we" are the church...So the question might more properly be, "Have we as Christians become sideline?" Have we lost our nerve? Have we forgotten our story as the children of God and become intimidated by principalities and powers? Have we become a chaplain to "the establishment" rather than a catalyst to society? Are we a church which has settled for maintenance rather than the mission to which our Lord calls us? ✠

THE RESPONSIBILITY OF GOVERNMENT
Diocese of Northwest Texas Convention, October 29, 1994

What we did at the General Convention of 1994, in effect, was to discover once again that the things that unite us are more important than the things that divide us. Despite deep disagreements over sexuality and how to handle conflict about ordained women, the Convention agreed to "continue the dialogue" rather than press for final answers which would inevitably have excluded people on one side or another.

The House of Deputies, I can tell you, was simply superb! The tone and feeling were the best I have ever seen. Time and again, deputies listened respectfully to each other, despite sometimes passionate disagreements. With persistence and patience they sought God's will for this Church and our mission in the world—through the hearings and committee process, in crafting effective legislation, during debate on the floor, and in their voting.

We sought to root ourselves in corporate worship, in Bible-sharing and theological reflection, in the loving discipline of daily Eucharistic fellowship. We met at the crossroads of Indianapolis—where more segments of interstate highways meet than anywhere else in the nation—and found among ourselves a rich diversity of gifts and the intersection of many profound but different experiences of God's saving grace. We struggled to hear each other across our differences, and to be faithful to the one God who binds us together through Christ's saving action and enlivens us through one

Holy Spirit. We sought to serve you, who entrusted us with the responsibility for the governance of our beloved Church, by being faithful to the Apostles' teaching and fellowship, in the breaking of bread and in prayer—that our decisions might further the Good News of Christ, the saving mission to which God calls us. ☩

"THE STATE OF THE CHURCH"
IN A TIME OF TRIAL
Synod of Province II, May 9, 1996

Leadership—and the perceived lack thereof—is often a topic in church circles (and national politics) these days. There are some good reasons for this, and some not so good reasons. I'd like to use leadership as a sort of "theme" for looking at some of the major issues that loom large in our church life today.

AFTERMATH OF SUICIDE & EMBEZZLEMENT

A year ago at this time we were still reeling from the January suicide of the Bishop of Massachusetts, followed by revelations of his marital infidelities, and the discovery of the embezzlement of 2.2-million dollars by the Episcopal Church's Treasurer. The details were shocking. Perhaps even more unsettling was the blow to our corporate self-esteem by such a dramatic fall from grace by two highly-visible church leaders, and the scape-goating that followed: How could this happen in our church? Whose "fault" is it? Someone must be to blame!

More than one group proclaimed that the Presiding Bishop and the rest of the "national church" leadership must be the source of the problem, and it became fashionable to call for Bishop Browning's resignation, as though he had stolen the money and encouraged someone else's adultery.

That is one of the burdens of leadership, I've discovered. When things go wrong, it must be the leader's fault. Let's throw the rascals out and then everything will be okay again.

Leaders do make mistakes, fall from grace, sin egregiously from time to time—being human like everybody else. But it seems to me that we have become increasingly eager to blame our leaders as the pace of change and the uncertainties of the future increase. There is a big difference between holding people accountable and scape-goating, but in our anxiety we often lose sight of it.

This concerns me personally, because I don't enjoy being a target for free-floating anxiety. But it concerns me even more because I think we must find healthier ways to manage our distress, our fear and our anger—individually and as a community. Everything we know suggests that change is not going to stop but will accelerate. Everything we believe tells us that God calls us to journey into the unknown, and that complaining to Moses about the food does not help us get there.

Learning from Scandal

From the embezzlement we've learned once again how necessary it is to be good stewards, to maintain checks and balances vigilantly, to audit thoroughly, never to allow financial power to become concentrated in the hands of one person. No one is immune to temptation.

The new Treasurer has put a fine team in place and they are rapidly rebuilding the safeguards which had been dismantled. I feel very confident about our new financial leadership. Closer attention to prudent financial management is going on elsewhere too. The embezzlement served as a wake-up call for many dioceses and parishes throughout the country who had not given recent attention to their accounting procedures. I hope we will also learn from this painful situation that the Body of Christ is not strengthened by adopting a self-righteous attitude—whether to condemn the woman caught with her hand in the offering plate or to blame her superiors.

Taking steps to prevent future embezzlements is a fairly straight-forward task. Dealing with sexual immorality on the part of a bishop is much more complicated. In Massachusetts, the man put himself beyond our ability to seek reconciliation, and the diocese has had to struggle for healing in his absence. Now, we learn that Maine—and the rest of us—must come to terms with the revelation of another bishop's infidelity. I have no doubt that other wretched situations involving bishops and leading clergy will also come to light. Again, some are eager to blame our "national leadership" for the presence of sin in high places. Let me suggest another way to look at this.

SIN IS NOT NEW; HOW WE HANDLE IT IS

The bishops of Massachusetts and Maine are not the first to succumb to sexual temptation or abuse of power. History is full of such incidents, but most of them never became public scandals because they were hidden. The victims were disbelieved, hushed up, bought off. The offenders either got away with it completely, or were quietly transferred or pensioned off. Standing Committees knew but were sworn to confidentiality. Rumors circulated, but we certainly never issued press releases that named names and held a bishop accountable for private behavior. We didn't want to ruin careers. We propped up the fiction that leaders don't fail the way the rest of us do.

That is what has changed. We don't pretend anymore, and we've dropped the double-standard. We don't trivialize sexual misconduct by calling it an "indiscretion" to be overlooked. We hold people accountable for their behavior instead of trying to protect reputations. We proclaim that we are a community of reconciliation that values truth, humility and repentance, and believes in the possibility of forgiveness, conversion, and new life.

This is very new behavior for us as a church, and it doesn't come easily. It's humiliating for all the world to know that our spiritual leaders are weak flesh and blood. We feel betrayed and angry if it's someone we respected, or counted on to lead the church in directions we want to go. We take smug pleasure if it's someone we didn't like or disagreed with. We're quick to throw stones, because condemning others helps us avoid examining ourselves. We prefer pointing at our neighbor's mote to admitting there's a beam in our own eye. But Christ has shown another way of justice transformed by mercy, and I trust we will continue to struggle along that path.

Individually and in tandem with our ecumenical partners, Episcopalians are struggling to discover what kind of a church God is calling us to be as we approach the third millennium of the Christian era. It's tempting to long for a charismatic leader who will rally everyone and set a 21st century church in motion—a sort of ecclesiastical Lee Iaccoca. But I wonder how much we would actually trust someone who came along with a detailed plan all ready to implement. Plans can be developed by any group of reasonably competent people if they share a vision of what is to be done.

VISION BEARERS

Archbishop Brian Davies of New Zealand has said that "church leaders need to see themselves as vision bearers, not problem solvers." We must be vision bearers first. Our task is to be open to God's presence among us as the pre-requisite for corporate discernment of God's will. We can only do that if we can suspend our own agendas and let the vision of God's agenda take shape in our hearts and minds. Then we can be problem solvers. Until then, we cannot even accurately recognize what the problems are.

As you prepare for the responsibilities many of you will carry to the General Convention, I urge you to focus first on the story, the vision, the flame. Then hold up the proposals, resolutions and concerns you are asked to consider to the light of that vision. We don't need lots of resolutions in order to be the Church God calls us to be. Rather we need a lot of love and prayer and conversation. Let's be a community of grace, confident that God will work through our political and parliamentary processes.

Finally, let's remember that this is God's church, not ours. We have an important role to play in our time, as others have had before us and will have after us. But the survival of the Church is not in our hands, and the redemption of the world is the responsibility of one far better qualified than we. Our faith and hope comes from knowing that God's plan of salvation is already being implemented. All we have to do is cooperate. JESUS has already been raised from the dead. All we have to do is say, ALLELUIA! ✠

LIVING FROM GOD'S ABUNDANCE

Executive Council, Toronto, Ontario, November 9,1996
Joint Meeting with Anglican Church of Canada

I expect we will find a lot of our assumptions turned on their heads as we live into new forms of community across political and ecclesiastical borders. We may have to give up some cherished aspects of our institutional self-image. We may have to modify, or even give up completely, some elements of our organization and some treasured traditions. But I also suspect—in fact, I firmly believe—that every treasure we relinquish in faith will be transformed and returned to us many times over. To live out of God's abundance is to be free of the limits of our own poverty.

I am reminded of a brief but powerful homily Barnum McCarty shared with my Council of Advice at just about this time in the last triennium. His text was the feeding of the multitude, and he drew a dramatic contrast between the responses of the disciples and the responses of Jesus to the situation. From the disciples came a triple negative:

1) it's not our problem,
2) we don't have the resources to address it,
3) the resources of others are woefully inadequate.

Jesus, by contrast, accepted responsibility for responding to the problem, instructed the disciples to inventory all available resources, and offered the meager results to God for a blessing. That faithful act of accountability and thanksgiving was all that was needed for God to perform the miracle.

That is surely an apt analogy for our responsibilities as leaders in the Church. Will we acknowledge the hunger of those around us? Do we trust each other enough to expose the meagerness of our own resources? Do we trust God to turn our scarcity into abundance?

BREAD THAT MUST BE BROKEN

Some aspects of our present institutional structures will probably turn out to be bread that must be broken in order to multiply. I don't know what that will look like in organizational terms—within ECUSA or the Anglican Communion, or with our ecumenical partners. Twentieth century bureaucracies which reflected the hierarchical structures of sky scrapers and office towers will be superseded by new patterns reflecting the horizontal networks of mutual ministry and electronic communications.

How that will evolve is still unclear. We need to be wary of projecting present models onto larger and larger international and ecumenical constellations of program and governance. We must also resist the temptation simply to dismantle current, centralized bureaucracies in a nostalgic search for some mythical simpler time. Living into the future is necessarily unnerving, because by definition we have to make it up as we go along. But as people of God, we have the assurance of clouds by day and pillars of fire by night. God does not leave us to stumble in darkness, and God will work the miracle if we are humble enough to offer thanks for the few loaves and fishes we can identify amidst a world of need.

A SOMBER REMINDER

I remain essentially an optimist, full of what I trust is hope in God's promises rather than foolish naiveté. As Christians we are called to live out our baptismal promises day by day—and that includes, day after day, resisting evil, renouncing "Satan and the spiritual forces of wickedness that rebel against God," renouncing "the evil powers of this world which corrupt and destroy the creatures of God."

Anyone who doubts the reality of those evil powers and their ability to corrupt God's children hasn't been paying much attention to what is going on in the world, or in the church. With sickening frequency we have witnessed spectacular sins involving money, sex, and the abuse of privilege and power. The widow's mite has been stolen; priests and bishops have violated trust and desecrated sanctuaries; this group and that arrogantly condemn each other as destroyers of the communion we know God wills for us.

None of us is as innocent as we might like to believe. None of us is as guilty as others might like to believe. The desire to scapegoat is primitive and powerful. Who wouldn't like to load all the evil that sullies the community of the church onto some spectacular villain we can drive from our midst to restore purity and peace.

But we are followers of Jesus Christ. He has already borne

our sins, all of them. To scapegoat feminists or homosexuals, or those who read the Bible differently than we do, or those who are afraid of changing roles or language or new modes of worship, or those who are blind to the riches of tradition, or those who think they own the Truth, or those who think there is no "Truth"—all that blaming simply distracts us from the task of the Church in every age: to be a community that stands on the far side of the Cross, never doubting its evil power but always proclaiming the far greater power of the Resurrection. ✠

Stewards of Food that Endures

Program, Budget & Finance Meeting, March 11, 1997

I feel sorry for the disciples in today's gospel (John 6:16-27). Jesus has just dazzled everyone by feeding 5000 people with 5 loaves and 2 fish. Then he does a vanishing act, leaving them to deal with a boisterous crowd who want to make Jesus king. So the disciples make their own escape by boat, rowing furiously across the lake. Jesus turns up again, miraculously, acting like nothing has happened.

After they get to the other shore, the crowd tracks them down again, and Jesus starts scolding: "All you want is food for your bellies," he says. "You keep misunderstanding the signs! Work only for the food which endures." How are the disciples to know what to do when their leader is so unpredictable, so mysterious? Why did he put them through the extraordinary exercise of feeding all those people from practically nothing and then blame them for being hungry? What is the "food that endures"?

TENSION BETWEEN SPIRITUALITY
AND JUSTICE-MAKING

I feel sorry for the disciples because I identify with them so often. As leaders among today's disciples we can easily get just as confused as the first ones did. Look at the tension apparent in this story between spirituality and justice-making. Jesus obviously believes in feeding the hungry, healing the sick, bringing in the outcast, and resisting the structures that perpetuate hunger, rob us of wholeness, and divide us from each other. But the gospel warns us about keeping these good works in perspective.

We are bound by the example of Christ to continue faithfully our ministries of service and care, our programs of outreach and education. We are also bound by the witness of today's gospel not to let these vital activities become ends in themselves. We must not confuse what we do with what and who and whose we are.

To be who we are is to keep centered in "the apostles' teaching and fellowship, in the breaking of bread, and in the prayers." All our good works must flow out of our faithfulness in Word and Sacrament, the food that endures, nourishing our individual spiritual growth as it binds us together in community. That's why we are here now, sustaining our fellowship through the breaking of bread and the prayers.

The Church has entrusted us with the awesome task of allocating our material resources for the combined tasks of witness and service to the world, and of maintaining our own common life. It's a hard job. Tensions and disagreements are inevitable. But even when we feel most beleaguered and at sea, Jesus will come walking into our midst and lead the way back to shore, and he will show us the difference between the food that perishes and the food that endures. We can trust in that. ✠

CHALLENGES OF CHURCH
LEADERSHIP TODAY

1997 Report and Proposal from Executive Council

Very few of us were around when the Council was first created in 1919. Most of today's members were not yet Episcopalians (or even alive!) at the beginning of the era of full-time Presiding Bishops. During the tenure of six great leaders of this church—Henry St. George Tucker, Henry Knox Sherrill, Arthur Lichtenberger, John Hines, John Allin and Edmond Browning—ECUSA membership has fluctuated from 2.27-million in 1945 through almost 3.6-million in the booming 50's and 60s, settling back to about 2.5-million today. Average congregation size has grown from 290 to 340, but we are actually distributed among a small number of very large congregations and a large number of small ones.

About 7,500 congregations are distributed among domestic dioceses which have increased from 74 plus 15 missionary districts to 100 full-fledged dioceses, under the spiritual leadership of bishops who have more than doubled in number from 153 to about 350 today. Relentless inflation has outstripped our stewardship, and major population shifts have played havoc with parochial "borders" so that a rising percentage of congregations can no longer afford full-time ordained leadership, even as the number of clergy has risen from 6,500 to more than 15,000.

CHANGES IN THE CHURCH COUNCIL SERVES

In our lifetimes, this church, like the world we are called to serve, has undergone truly immense changes, and this shows no sign of abating. Change always creates anxiety and puts stress on organizational structures. Increasing attentiveness to voices previously ignored or silenced has challenged the church to re-examine many assumptions that undergird our institutional life. In this process, shared faith and deepening sense of community offer a grace-filled balance as tension and conflict increase. The present Executive Council has done its best to keep its work rooted in worship and the Word, responsive to the many different voices of faithful Episcopalians, and courageous in witnessing—in word and deed—to God's love and justice in a world sorely lacking both. I would love to know what historians of the late 21st century will say about our stewardship of the Episcopal Church in the closing days of the Second Millennium. Being a leader is not easy in the church today. I doubt that the early church fathers and mothers had an easy time of it either.

What the historians may say will be, in the end, of little import. Council members, like all Christians, must work not for worldly success or approbation but for the glory of God, and there is only one judge we need hope will look mercifully on us. We are stewards for a season, but the Body of Christ is in far more capable hands than our own. So we do the best we know how, and trust the Holy Spirit to bring all to completion. ✠

DOING WHAT DOES NOT COME NATURALLY

Executive Council Eucharist,
February 16, 1998, San Jose, California

The Gospel often makes me uneasy, a little irritated. Maybe chagrined is the right word. I don't really like being reminded of all those hard sayings: bless those who persecute you, live in harmony with one another, don't be haughty, don't repay evil with evil, lay down your life, love one another.

They sound wonderful, of course, those hard sayings. They roll off our tongues easily because they are so familiar. But doing them is another matter, and I really don't like being reminded about it. It's challenge enough to live in harmony with the people I like. Blessing those who persecute me does not come naturally. Loving everyone does not come naturally, especially when it means being willing to give up my life—my preferences and prejudices, my comforts and commitments, my goals and dreams.

It does not come naturally to set them all aside in order to be present with everyone: every single "other" I may encounter, every person, in or out of the Church, who crosses my path or writes a nasty letter, every child of God—including those who appear to be "enemies" busily persecuting the institutions and the people I cherish. What a hard saying that God calls me to love like this! I hate being reminded of it.

SAVING GRACE

I hate being reminded of it, because I have no faith in my ability to do it. In fact, I know that I cannot do it. You cannot do it. None of us can live this way, except by the grace of God. That's the reassurance, if you will; the saving grace. We become able to live into these hard sayings because we have the amazing privilege of being "friends" of Jesus Christ, and Jesus promises that the Father will give us what we need to follow his commands.

"You did not choose me but I chose you," Jesus says. Why choose those particular disciples, with all their obvious flaws and weaknesses? What about the skills and talents needed for leadership? What about administrative experience and managerial expertise? Why did Jesus choose a handful of rough working people, not very educated or articulate, impetuous, ambitious, cowardly, stubborn and wrong-headed, painfully slow to catch on to what he was saying and doing? Were there no others in Galilee more suitable for the task?

And why us? Are we really any more suitable? Yet God chooses us, now, to lead our little corner of the Church, and charges us with the same tasks of loving, living in harmony, blessing those who persecute us. And Jesus promises that we will be given what we need to live into these hard sayings.

CONFLICT AND DIVISION

Conflict and division in the Church are not a modern invention. Over and over again, these words of Jesus have been applied by our predecessors in the Church, facing their own versions of the troubles we experience now. Over and over again, Christians have disagreed about what God required of them. Over and over again, the Church has shuddered and splintered and split on the hard rock of human error and sin. Over and over again, chastened followers of Jesus Christ have struggled for healing and reconciliation amidst the wreckage of our favorite institutional structures and ideological frameworks.

As Bishop Griswold said at his investiture, the words St. Francis heard from Christ on the Cross, "Repair my church," are spoken to us as well. In every generation Christ calls men and women to repair and restore the community of faith. Like Francis in his time, and countless others since then and yet to come, we are called to repair the fraying bonds of trust and commitment that bind us within the one Body of Christ — over and over and over again.

We cannot respond effectively to that call if we allow our attention to be held captive by the problems. If we concentrate on what's wrong, we will be trapped in frustration and anger and bitterness. "Do not repay anyone evil for evil, but take thought for what is noble in the sight of all," Paul tells the Romans. "Take thought for what is noble in the sight of all."

We must fasten our attention on the one who died and rose again for us, whom we meet in Scripture, and encounter in this sacrament of the Eucharist; whom we meet among the poor and needy, and encounter in the hearts of fellow Episcopalians of every liturgical and theological preference.

If we focus anxiously on our disagreements and discord and divisions, it will be very difficult—perhaps impossible—to see God or to live in harmony with one another. If we keep our eyes on the risen Christ, we will recognize the unity already given to us, and be shown how to restore the Body to wholeness. We know that God wills the Good News to be preached to every generation. Of course it doesn't come naturally to bless those who persecute us, or to give up our lives, our preferences, our dreams. Of course it doesn't come naturally to set aside our prejudices and commitments to be present with every single "other" we encounter.

But by the grace of God in Christ Jesus we are set free from our individual and corporate sins to love and serve one another. By the power of the Holy Spirit we shall receive wisdom and courage to repair the Church in our own time as our forebears did before us. ☫

SAINTS CHALLENGE US

Washington National Cathedral, All Saints, 1998

We are all called to be saints, all of us today, just as Christians from the beginning have been called to be saints—to be the "blessed" of the beatitudes. Most of us don't do it very well, but sainthood has never been a hundred-percent-or-nothing sort of thing. Only God is 100%. The rest of us may aspire to perfection, but even the best fall short. Not one stained glass hero or heroine was perfect; neither are we excused from seeking to be saints.

That's what the religious tradition is all about. It preserves for us the stories of the countless men and women who have gone before, who have encountered the living God and let that encounter transform their lives so that God's love could be made known to others. It preserves these stories not as quaint or interesting bits of history, but as example, inspiration, model for our own lives.

We are not free to read about them, close the book, and walk away. Their lives call us to decision, to wrestle with how to apply the Gospel to the particularities of our own life and times, as they did in theirs. We are called to do this as individuals, generation after generation. We are also called to do this as the Church, as one era succeeds another in our institutional life.

20TH CENTURY DEVELOPMENTS, AND THEN?

Episcopalians at the end of the twentieth century can look back on several decades of extraordinary developments in our institutional life:

- women's participation in church government;
- the ordination of women as deacons, priests and bishops;
- a revised prayer book
- the enrichment of our worship with non-Anglo music and new liturgical texts;
- the Eucharist as our central act of worship with its powerful symbols of being gathered, fed, and sent forth to do God's will;
- a growing openness to the testimony of God's action in the lives of our gay and lesbian members,
- our stumbling but persistent efforts to respond to both personal and institutional racism.

That Nathan Baxter is the Dean, Jane Dixon is the Bishop Suffragan, and I am in this pulpit, would have been wildly inconceivable forty or even thirty years ago. The Church definitely has a new face.

But what of the road ahead? What are we being called to bring about in the next generation, the next century, the next millenium, that may seem wildly inconceivable today? After what aspects of righteousness ought we to hunger and thirst? In the midst of what conflicts are we to stand as peace-makers? How shall we, as affluent Americans, become poor in spirit among the hungry and desperate all over this planet?

Each of us, as individuals, must ask ourselves these questions. The Church, too, must ask these questions, in our governing councils and conventions, and in all the offices and departments and program groups through which we carry out mission and ministry.

Will the saints we remember today recognize, acknowledge and claim us as fellow pilgrims in the 2000-year parade of those who follow Jesus Christ? Will our lives and contributions be remembered by those who come after us, as worthy bearers of the Christian tradition? May God give us grace to recognize our call, to pass through the great ordeal, and to bear the good news of Christ's Resurrection as worthy successors to those who have gone before us. ✠

THE TRANSFIGURATION SYNDROME
St. Andrew's Church, Denver, Colorado, February 24, 1999

Peter, James and John were witnesses to the Transfigura-tion, including the images of Moses and Elijah talking with Jesus. What a conversation! Moses who looked upon the face of God and lived; Elijah who was carried into God's presence in a chariot of fire; and Jesus, who brought God's presence right down to where we live and work and pray, and would soon harrow the very gates of Hell to reconcile us forever with our loving Creator.

What a conversation! It's no surprise that Peter once again blundered into it. Oh, this is so amazing and wonderful, he says. Oh, we're so lucky to have seen this! Let's mark the spot so others will know. Let's build three dwellings, or tents, or booths (depending on your translation), sacred places to commemorate this sacred moment, so others can come here to pray and connect with this awesome experience.

It was a noble intention, but God's response was a blinding light and a terrifying voice: "This is my Son, listen to him!" Peter's blunder on the mountaintop stands as a caution to Christians down through the ages, especially to those who are active in the church, who hold responsible positions in the parish, or the diocese, or the national church.

We need structure. We need shelter. We need a framework for our lives together. We need dwellings and tents and booths, where we can feel safely at home, where we can teach our children the Good News, where we can be reminded of the glimpse of glory that is ours when we come into God's presence. But we are always in danger of taking something that seems wonderful at the time and freezing it for all time.

We need the institution of the Church to guide us on our individual pilgrimages, to carry the story from one generation to another, to inspire us with words and music and soaring architecture and the traditions of all the generations who have gone before us. We need structures to organize our lives, and enable us to use resources efficiently, and provide continuity and stability to our common life.

But we must be very, very careful not to succumb to the "transfiguration syndrome." Peter was so intent on capturing and preserving one glorious moment that he lost sight of the living Christ right there in front of him. "This is my Son. Listen to him." We must not be so intent on preserving the structures of the Church that we lose sight of the living Christ who meets us day after day in those around us.

FROM TENTS TO CORNERSTONE

There are many ministries to support, missionaries to recruit and deploy and sustain, educational resources to develop and distribute, partnerships with dioceses and provinces and other Anglican bodies around the world to maintain, a budget to manage and a new one to prepare, staff to train and pay and provide with benefits—there are a lot of tasks involved in our stewardship of the affairs of the church.

General Convention, diocesan councils, vestries and committees of all sorts are stewards of the life and work and resources of the church, with a sacred obligation to protect the institution so it can continue to carry the Gospel to the next generation. But how easy it is to lose sight of God's glory in the midst of such responsibilities. How easy it is to want to freeze things just as they were when we first heard God's call. How hard it is to give up our reliance on structures and institutions and procedures and buildings and trust instead in the transfiguring power of Jesus Christ.

Peter was impulsive, but he wasn't a fool. Jesus knew this, and made Peter the cornerstone of the church: Peter, the Rock—much more enduring than any tent he could have put up on the Mount of Transfiguration. Peter was not supposed to build the church just then. That could happen only after Christ's passion and death and resurrection. The moment of the Transfiguration gave the disciples an inkling of the full glory of the resurrected Christ; but between the two lay the long, suffering path leading to the Cross.

We who love the Church must walk that long path too, confident that if we listen to God's beloved Son we will be sustained on the journey, and at its end will see face to face not dwellings or tents or booths, not buildings or prayer books or conventions, but the most high and ever-loving God, made known to us in Christ Jesus, living within us through the Holy Spirit. ✠

BUREAUCRATIC TEMPTATIONS
Executive Council, Fond du Lac, Wisconsin, June 14, 1999

It's so easy to get caught up in bureaucratic concerns. Yes, of course, we must be attentive and responsible about finances and program effectiveness and personnel policies and computer systems and all the other administrative aspects which undergird the mission of the church.

And yet it is most refreshing to meet so many people in pew after pew, so to speak, whose concerns have nothing to do with assessments or parochial reports or the finer points of canon law, but rather with how to live a Christian life in today's world, how the Church can help them raise good children, or deal with serious illness or aging parents, or cope with tragic accidents, or bring stewardship ideals to bear on a local environmental conflict.

This is the challenge always before us, to balance care for the institution of the Church, Christ's Body, with commitment to the mission of the Church, to bring the reconciling love of Christ to all the world.

Members of the General Convention, the Executive Council, and the staff of the Episcopal Church Center, have been called by the church to special responsibilities for the institution itself. But if we don't keep the primary mission foremost in mind, we risk turning our structures into idols and undermining the very work we are meant to support. ✠

ORGANIZATIONAL RENEWAL
Episcopal Church Club of Philadelphia, September 21, 1999

The God we worship and the Good News of the Gospel are the same yesterday, today and forever. But the Church's organization has had to adapt itself from one era to the next. The Episcopal Church is in the midst of another cycle of organizational renewal just now. It is disorienting and a bit frightening, as well as exciting and full of promise.

For most of the 1990's, General Convention and the church press have given much attention to questions about institutional structure. A major theme that keeps resurfacing is a desire to move away from a "centralized bureaucracy" toward a "network" of ministries, away from "national programs" to support for diocesan and local programs. We are steadily living into the commitments of the Baptismal Covenant, which call each of us to active involvement in the worship and ministry of the Body of Christ. This takes different forms in different areas, reflecting the increasing cultural diversity of both the church and the society.

A GOOD TIME TO BE ALIVE

All of this makes our generation a particularly challenging but wonderful time to be alive. God has called us to worship and service at a vital transition point in the life of the Church. We see some of what is happening already: I wouldn't be standing here as President of the House of Deputies, and no women clergy would be in the room, if some pretty big changes had not already taken place.

What is still to happen is not so clear, but we ought to expect continuing changes: in organizational structure, in language, in the way we incorporate new members and nurture our children, in our understanding of the mutual ministry of laity and clergy, men and women, in the degree of welcome we extend to those "different" from the "norm," in the way we share our financial resources to support Christ's mission on earth. ☩

Courteous almost to a fault, President Chinnis is keenly aware of the value of politeness in politics, of civility in building community. She values the structures that create shared expectations about roles and relationships, and prizes the discipline and generosity which enabled 800+ deputies to handle hundreds of resolutions, and the conflicts some of them engendered, in a loving Christian spirit. Order can create space for discovering our unity in Christ, and developing a community of respect in a time of conflict and change.

Decency: Common Sense and Community

FINDING A COMMON GROUND: HOW DO WE LIVE WITH DIFFERENCES?

Diocese of Chicago Convocation, March 16, 1996

In the temple story, the Pharisee was so fixated on gaining approval by following the rules that he forgot that GOD's love is free, that God's mercy cannot be earned, that it is not our own self-discipline or sacrifice or good behavior but Jesus who saves us from our sins.

That is the basis for our common ground, I think: the realization that we are all in need of GOD's mercy. The Pharisee must leave his place of privilege and join the tax collector in the place of sorrow and repentance. This is very, very hard to do. And that roaring lion, the devil, seems especially eager to prevent us from doing it. Just when we try our hardest to stake out a common meeting place, he comes snarling around with bad breath and sharp claws to run us off.

Dwelling together in unity is very hard work. It's impossibly hard if we try to do it by ourselves. With his own eyes, the Pharisee can never see anything but a contemptible tax collector when he looks at his brother across the temple. But God invites us to see Christ in that other. Doing so, we can learn to see with Christ's eyes, the eyes of love and forgiveness and infinite patience—but it is not easy, not at first, and not even after seventy times seven. It is not easy, yet we are called again and again to try.

A PAINFUL EXAMPLE

Let me give you a concrete example of how difficult it is, and how necessary, and how ultimately full of blessing it can be to seek out that common ground:

One of the duties of the President of the House of Deputies is to appoint the clergy and laity who serve on the various committees, commissions, boards and agencies that work between General Conventions. I must also appoint the deputies who make up all the Legislative Committees, which prepare and make recommendations on resolutions at the Convention itself.

There are about 200 appointments to be made each triennium to the interim bodies, and more than 400 deputies are appointed to Legislative Committees. The canons place certain restrictions in terms of the number of clergy and laity to be appointed, and generally require, or at least encourage broad geographical representation. It's very challenging, under tight time pressures, to match the skills and interests of so many people with the responsibilities of 30-plus interim bodies and 26 Legislative committees.

When I became President, I promised myself that I would work to broaden the make-up of these groups to reflect the diversity of the Church in more than just geographic terms. Because of our history as a part of Western culture, it has been a mostly-white, mostly-male subset of the Church making decisions for everyone, for a very long time. I wanted the policy recommendations from interim bodies, and the legislative recommendations from convention committees, to draw on the perspectives of women and of people from different racial and ethnic groups, different age groups, different points of view, in addition to the wisdom and experience of those who have been involved in our leadership for decades.

I have a very high view of the political process as a mechanism through which the Spirit works in the Church. I wanted that process to be as wide open as possible, so we could catch the wind of the Spirit no matter which way it blows. I wanted to make sure that people who had been excluded from our decision-making processes in the past, sometimes intentionally, would in future be included. So I cast my net in many directions, asking groups wherever I went to make recommendations for appointments.

In the summer of 1993, in the early stages of gathering names for appointments for the 1994 Convention's legislative committees, I addressed the national convention of Integrity and repeated my request for recommendations. You may have seen some of the attacks that followed that address. I was accused of misusing my office. I was accused of stacking committees to promote a "gay agenda." I was accused of abusing the power to appoint by excluding those opposed to Integrity.

FACING THE PHARISEE WITHIN

My first reaction was hurt and anger. I was not excluding anyone, but trying to include those I knew my predecessor had deliberately refused to appoint. How could I "stack" 26 committees with six openly-gay or lesbian deputies? Why was it a misuse of my office to encourage honest dialogue and debate, and to invite everyone to take part? In fact, my first impulse was to retaliate, to go ahead and do what they were accusing me of doing and not appoint anyone with so-called "traditionalist" views about women or sexuality. The little Pharisee in my head said, "Thank GOD I'm not like those intolerant people! I'm certainly not going to appoint any of them...." The hot breath of that prowling lion was right on my neck.

What saved me from being devoured was the other little voice that said, "GOD, be merciful to me, a sinner." Maybe I had not done enough to let the other "others" know of my intent to include everyone. At least, the message didn't seem to have gotten across. Maybe I had not loved my traditionalist brothers and sisters enough to anticipate that my words of invitation to Integrity might sound like words of rejection to Episcopalians United or the Synod. Maybe it looked as though I were trying to move the church's flag onto some foreign territory, instead of raising it higher to draw more people in.

So I bit my tongue and redoubled my efforts to appoint conservatives as well as liberals, men and women, straight and gay, white and black and Hispanic and Asian and native American, charismatics and anglo-catholics, lawyers and homemakers, old and young—all the rainbow people of GOD. So far, I have only been partially successful, because our system still favors certain categories of Episcopalians over others, and perhaps because some are still suspicious of my motives and believe I will black-ball conservatives so they don't bother to put names forward.

But there is more diversity than there used to be. And it is a good thing. How much better that we work on our differences by talking with each other, instead of about each other. How much better that we learn to sit across the table and see each other as fellow creatures of the one true GOD, instead of letting the prowling lion convince us that the real devil is that person who looks or thinks or loves differently than I do.

TAKING THE RISK, BEARING THE DISCOMFORT

It has not always been easy for my appointees to sit down with each other. It's awkward to work with someone who approaches things in a very very different way. It's hard not being able to assume we all agree about the things that really matter. But I believe that it is precisely when we are willing to take that risk and bear that discomfort that the SPIRIT is set free to work among us.

One of the most moving moments at the 1994 General Convention came on the last of our ten hard days of work, when three members of the Legislative Committee on Social and Urban Affairs asked, as a point of personal privilege, to make a statement. Del Glover of Delaware, Louie Crew of Newark, and Judy Mayo of Fort Worth rose together to thank Earl Cavanaugh of Kansas City for his leadership of that most controversial of committees (1994 Journal, p.817). A black man, a gay man and a woman from the ESA rose to express their love and respect for the straight white man who had shepherded them through debates on dozens of sensitive issues.

I don't think there was a person on the floor of the House of Deputies who wasn't affected by that witness to the power of claiming our common ground. The differences among members of that committee symbolized by those four gave a richness and thoroughness to the committee's deliberations that enabled it to bring well-crafted recommendations to the House, enriching our work and making it much more efficient. More than that, their obvious camaraderie and affection demonstrated better than any sermon the power of GOD to bridge our differences and make us one in the Body in CHRIST. All the grief and criticism that had accompanied the appointment process was suddenly worth it.

I will never forget that moment; and I invite you to think of similar moments in your own life in this church, when those on opposing sides of important issues have been willing to meet together, to work together, as fellow believers in JESUS CHRIST seeking GOD's will for the Church. It's hard work. It can open us up to lots of misunderstanding and criticism. But now and then we are graced with a glimpse of how blessed it is for brothers and sisters to live together in unity. Now and then we are able to see plainly that the things which bind us together are far deeper and stronger than those which divide us. Now and then we experience the power of GOD to overcome our suspicion and isolation and fear. Now and then the SPIRIT catches us, and carries us to a new place we could not have dreamed about. ✠

SEEKING A COMMON MIND

*Fellows Conference, College of Preachers,
Washington, D.C., April 1996*

At the 1994 General Convention, there were some resolutions which ended up being substantially amended by debate, changed by one House after the other had voted so that conference committees were necessary to try to find a compromise, or in a few cases ultimately rejected by one House despite approval in the other. These were in every case resolutions dealing with issues about which we do not yet have a clear consensus or "common mind" of the church.

Things like revising our structure, the place of those who reject women's ordination, and human sexuality, proved difficult or impossible to legislate—and that is as it should be. The parliamentary system of debate ensures that all voices can be heard, and our very conservative process of voting by orders on major questions prevents rushing to decisions before a substantial consensus has been reached. Unanimity is rarely possible—but the legislative process gives us a dynamic framework for seeking GOD'S will amidst the wealth of contributions from many perspectives.

The conduct of everyone in the House of Deputies in Indianapolis, even when dealing with very painful topics, gave me great hope—even joy—about the state of our life together. There was a civility of debate, a generosity of spirit, a respect for other points of view, a willingness to listen, and to really hear each other, that I found very heartening.

Our bishops seem to be passing through a more difficult period in their life. In part because they are so much smaller a body—200+ compared to almost 900—and get to know each other so well through frequent meetings during their life-long service, they seem to have trouble switching into the structured decision-making mode required by our triennial legislative calendar.

I also became aware of a significant difference in attitude toward Convention between bishops and deputies: every single deputy wants to be there. No one runs for election as deputy unless she or he is committed to the political process as an appropriate method for discerning GOD'S will in community, and actually likes participating in big busy events. Our bishops, on the other hand, have to be there whether they like meetings and politics or not. Not all of them are happy campers when we gather, and their personal discomfort affects their participation. For this reason, collaborative meetings of the Legislative Committees are particularly valuable, enabling deputies to share their skills and enthusiasm for the process. ☩

MESSINESS AS A COST OF FREEDOM

May 1996 Column in Episcopal Life

In 1996, I was privileged to travel to the Dominican Republic and Cuba with the Presiding Bishop, to visit and support our Anglican brothers and sisters in those countries. Visiting Cuba reminded me how much I, as a U.S. citizen and member of the Episcopal Church, tend to take for granted the freedoms, responsibilities and privileges of democracy. Suppose the Episcopal Church were governed by a dictator instead of the General Convention. Suppose decisions were made for us, instead of by us.

Our system of church governance is often messy, because a high level of agreement must be achieved before we make major changes in our common life. Because General Convention only meets every three years, we must often bear a lot of ambiguity between opportunities for decision-making. Lack of clear "answers" to urgent questions is profoundly troubling, from our human perspective. Yet I remain persuaded that God invites us to witness to our faith precisely in such ambiguity, and I would rather live with short-term messiness than tidy authoritarianism.

Only by being open to the multiple gifts and perspectives of everyone called into this community can we hope to glimpse the boundless reality of God's revelation. Our democratically-elected church councils and conventions, assuring the laity a strong voice alongside clergy, provide for expression, dialogue and debate about all these perspectives as the framework for our decision-making.

As I look back over our history, I have no doubt that the Holy Spirit uses our debates and conflicts, our legislative channels, and our parliamentary procedures to guide us in discerning God's will for the Church in our time. The political process may not be comfortable. It certainly requires a great deal of patience and charity. But it works. ✠

THE POLITICS OF STRUCTURE

Executive Council, Charleston, West Virginia, June 11, 1996

> *Conflicts about structure and budgets, and radical proposals to change them, are fueled by disagreements about other matters. We all know this but are usually reluctant to name it. I think we must. We must recognize this dynamic as part of the process, in order to make good decisions about structure and money.*
>
> *The traditionalists are clear about it. For years, traditionalist organizations have wielded financial clubs and tried to create alternative structures— a "church within the church"—whenever the established structures produced decisions they opposed. The Episcopal Synod of America has long sought an independent jurisdiction to protect its opposition to the ordination of women. The new American Anglican Congress takes a similar approach in connection with sexuality.*
>
> *Some of these efforts are responses to decisions of the whole General Convention, while others react to events in the House of Bishops. Minority bishops issued sharp protests following both the bishops' vote last fall about the acceptance of the ordination of women and last month's Righter court ruling, vowing to continue the search for alternative structures to avoid accepting the majority view, and*

naming diversion of funds as a tool in that process. They know that structure and money are both about the power to make decisions, decisions that shape what this Church is and how it will witness to the Gospel in our time. It's silly for the rest of us not to acknowledge the same thing.

Disagreements about policy based on conflicting theologies, and the resulting attacks on program, are inextricably entwined with debates about organizational and financial structures. Let's not be afraid to name this and deal with it forthrightly. Whatever "label" others might ascribe to our personal commitments, all of us have an interest in protecting the bonds between dioceses and the governing structure that enables us to function as the Episcopal Church in the USA.

There are threats to our unity from many sides. If we allow these to make us defensive, hostile or resistant to change, the institutional cost will be very high indeed. Instead, let's remember that our only true unity lies in the love of God, the hope of the resurrection, and the power of the Holy Spirit. Our call as leaders and stewards of the institutional church has meaning only if we hold fast to our primary identity as members of the Body of Christ. If we trust in that unity, surely God's grace will lead us to right decisions, no matter how painful the process. ✠

"ONE BODY, ONE SPIRIT, ONE HOPE"
Province III Convocation, Hagerstown, Maryland, July 1, 1996

No matter how painful our differences may be, I hope we will never forget that they are insignificant in the light of the redeeming love of GOD in CHRIST JESUS.

What unites us is far stronger and more lasting than what divides us. "There is one Body and one SPIRIT, just as you were called in the one hope of your calling." (Ephesians 4:4) We are called to serve as stewards of the institutional church in our generation, and it is a grave responsibility. But it is also a duty to be embraced with joyful hope and confidence. The Church is not ours but the Body of CHRIST, and we can trust the HOLY SPIRIT to guide us so that all our work gives glory to GOD and communicates the Good News of the Gospel to all who see us. ☦

WHATEVER HAPPENED TO POLITE BEHAVIOR?
Executive Council, Cincinnati, Ohio, January 1997

"Civility," as Ellen Goodman noted in a column earlier this month, "is all the rage." All sorts of people are commenting on the need for it—the lack of it—in church and society, in public and private, in the halls of Congress and church conventions, on the highways and across the supermarket check-out counter and over the airwaves, in schools and around kitchen tables and even over coffee in the parish hall.

When I was growing up, and for most of my adulthood, I lived in a world where standards of polite behavior were known, shared, accepted and honored. Violations, when they occurred, were shockingly offensive and rewarded with scorn, ostracism and a kind of pulling in of the community to protect itself against destructive interactions. Today, "shock jocks" make big money on radio, vulgarity and insult pass for humor on the sitcoms, and every day political and religious leaders substitute personal invective for reasoned persuasion in seeking support for their causes.

Have we become a nation of rude people, a church community without simple manners? What is going on here? And how should we respond to this state of affairs—as Christians called to "respect the dignity of every human being," and as Episcopalians approaching a General Convention that promises more than the usual share of contentious issues?

CIVILITY AND CONSENSUS

It's no secret that standards of behavior vary from place to place, culture to culture, century to century. What was polite in the 18th century French Court would seem odd in this 20th century hotel. Good manners in Maine might seem abrupt and rude in Georgia; Midwestern friendliness can appear intrusive or threatening in a New York subway.

To some degree, how we ought to behave toward each other is situational. It is relative, conditioned by external factors along with our internal disposition. It is okay (apparently) to scream "Kill 'em" in the excitement of the basketball play-offs, but not in the middle of debate in the House of Deputies. In some churches, blue jeans and sneakers are perfectly acceptable, while in others violation of a more formal dress code would be taken as a sign of disrespect for God and the community.

Knowing the difference, being able to judge which behaviors are appropriate in which situations, depends on sharing a lot of assumptions and expectations, many of them so ingrained in our upbringing that they remain quite unconscious. As long as we all have the same upbringing, things work out pretty well. We know automatically how to behave properly, and are likely to be offensive to others only when we lose our tempers, or—occasionally—when we're deliberately rude to make some sort of a point. As long as we all have the same upbringing—now there's the rub.

DECENTLY AND IN ORDER

Public life in this country used to be the preserve of the white upper class, who did share most of the same upbringing, values, interests and assumptions. Today, universal education and mass communication have dramatically expanded the range of acceptable behavior.

Life in the Episcopal Church used to be—or so the reigning mythology would have it—essentially the white upper class at prayer, snug in their box pews. Stately liturgies with their Elizabethan cadences defined the Episcopal way of worshipping, and of being with each other. Episcopalians did not cry out, "Praise the Lord!" in the middle of worship, and we didn't raise our voices in vestry meetings or the General Convention. There were disagreements aplenty, and Anglican history is as full of behind-the-scenes back-stabbings as any other. But publicly we were genteel. We were polite.

We behaved "decently and in order" because we shared an understanding of what "order" and "decency" were. It was a sort of Victorian understanding, dominated by Boston Brahmins and Southern gentlemen, and it held for a long time. It was strong enough—that behavioral consensus—to keep our ecclesial community essentially intact despite battles over candles and incense, slavery and temperance, suffrage and divorce.

Let other denominations thunder denunciations from pulpits and break into splinter groups right and left, north and south, orthodox and reformed. We prized civility and were rewarded with unity, we avoided open conflict and escaped schism. We finessed taking a position on slavery and were the only mainline denomination not to split before the

Civil War. The via media, the middle where the broad consensus held, was wide and strong.

THE LOSS OF CONCENSUS AND THE RISE OF FEAR

Now, we are not so confident about the consensus. The Episcopal Church is no longer dominated by Boston Brahmins and Southern gentleman with long Anglican memories and good Victorian manners. Voices previously unheard are speaking up, groups previously excluded are claiming a place in the Body of Christ. More and more people recognize that the comfortable old "consensus" was actually the preferences of a privileged few imposed on everyone else.

The civility that depended on shared experiences, interests and assumptions is stretched to the breaking point. Those who felt comfortable with the old ways feel very threatened. We are assailed by fears of change, the anxiety of facing the unknown, apprehension about a future we cannot see. It's hard to be civil when you are afraid. Yet we are called to love each other.

REDEFINING "CIVILITY"

Jesus was not always polite. He was not afraid to give offense, and his behavior sometimes scandalized. He did not say, "be polite and things will work out." He said, "love each other," "heal the sick," "feed my sheep."

We need to refresh our understanding of "civility." It does not mean having no conflicts, but managing our conflicts with compassion. It has never been just about politeness and seemly behavior, but about being good citizens. In our case that means being good citizens of the kingdom of God: speaking the truth, in love; bearing one another's burdens; not obsessing about the speck in our neighbor's eye while ignoring the log in our own.

If we go to General Convention expecting a showdown with winners and losers, we'll certainly get one, and it will be a colossal folly resulting from a great shared delusion, a consensus of fear. If we go to General Convention intent on one particular outcome—however earnest and conscientious our commitments may be—we will short-circuit the legislative process and undermine the peace and unity of the church.

This is easy to forget because we often think of the legislative process as a sort of civilized warfare: those who marshal the greatest electoral force can compel the rest to submit. Certainly it can be used in this way, and often is, in secular government as in the church.

But suppose we reframe the process. Suppose we see the legislative process not as civilized warfare—in which all the parties know from the start what territory they want to protect or reclaim—but as collaborative exploration, seeking an as-yet-unrecognized pathway through unfamiliar territory. Suppose we suspend our convictions long enough to listen for new clues about the path ahead, allowing for some new consensus that might embrace our present contradictions.

THE LEGISLATIVE PROCESS AS CHANNEL OF THE SPIRIT

Seen this way, the legislative process offers an orderly method for sharing information from scouts exploring in several different directions, testing it against our collective experience and wisdom, and making incremental decisions about next steps. It is in this sense that the legislative process can be the venue of the Holy Spirit's action within the Church. We are not totally on our own. We are not left to our own devices, jostling for position in fear of plunging into some ghastly pit. The territory is unfamiliar, but we are accompanied by one who has plumbed the abyss of death and returned in glory, promising to be with us always.

The Risen Christ does not promise easy agreements or simple solutions. Trusting the guidance of the Holy Spirit does not automatically cast out fear of the unknown. It is still hard work, with no guarantees. We will be exhausted when we leave. But let us struggle to recover the civility of the pure in heart, knowing it is essential to our souls and to the life of this church. It is a struggle, because we hunger for Truth with a capital "T" but fear disaster if we don't hold fast to the glimpse of truth we have already been given.

Let me close with an image I have found comforting as we prepare to take council together this summer. It comes from an Epiphany sermon by Dr. Margaret Guenther of General Seminary. Speaking of the journey of the magi, she reminded listeners that "you cannot see the star that shows the way unless you are willing to go into the night." We cannot see the star unless we go into the night, and we must leave behind our flashlights and our little torches—all our individual glimpses of truth—because they will only blind us to the fullness of Truth God has prepared for us.

This is the path to the reconciliation God wills—not facing each other in resolute dialogue determined to reach agreement at any cost, but walking side by side toward the One who reconciles all through the Peace that passes understanding. ✠

"CIVILITY" REVISITED

Diocese of Eastern Oregon Convention, October 1997

Before last summer's Convention, I said, *If we go to General Convention expecting a showdown with winners and losers, we'll certainly get one... If we go to Philadelphia intent on one particular outcome—however earnest and conscientious our commitments may be—we will short-circuit the legislative process and undermine the peace and unity of the church.*

Thanks be to God, most Bishops and Deputies allowed the convention process to work. In worship and Bible sharing, in committee meetings and legislative sessions, we sought God's will for the Episcopal Church for the next three years. One area in which consensus had eluded us for twenty years was clarified—this church does ordain women. In another—human sexuality—we agreed that there was still no consensus, and committed ourselves to continue to pray and study and talk with each other about it.

And we did it all in a calm and loving spirit. Testimony at hearings and debates on the floor demonstrated both the passion people had about issues and their resolve to express that passion with charity and patience. We deliberated and voted on a lot of difficult matters, and everyone—participant and observer alike—seems to agree that we did a pretty good job of acting like fellow Christians.

THE "NICE-ENE" CREED

Treating each other well apparently doesn't make for good headlines: one Philadelphia commentator bemoaned our "mind-numbing civility" and wondered how much commitment bishops and deputies might have to decisions made in such a restrained and polite manner. I say responding to God's passionate love for humankind does not require screaming at each other. I'm sorry if we disappointed the journalists, but I'm not sorry we were restrained and polite because that restraint and courtesy expressed our commitment to love God and each other. There were jokes in Philadelphia about the "Nice-ene" Creed, but most everyone was relieved to know they could count on an attentive hearing no matter how much their views might differ from the majority. It was good not to have to be armed for battle all the time.

I was immensely proud of the discipline and courage shown by members of the House of Deputies as they worked through a huge agenda, and pleased by what I have heard about the process in the House of Bishops. We are finding ways to work "in council" in a period when it is chiefly the love of God that holds us together rather than our agreement about particular issues. The consensus needed for "civility" in our dealings came from widespread awareness that we all love God and love this Church even when we radically disagree about certain matters. I am heartened by the commitment shown by so many to continue to work together in this way.

CONSENSUS IS NOT UNANIMITY

Not everyone shares that commitment. Some believe deeply that women cannot be ordained, that homosexual behavior is always wrong, and that the failure of General Convention to uphold traditional interpretations of Scripture on these matters is a gross violation of the will of God. Since Convention there have been several statements issued by groups holding such views, deploring what we did in Philadelphia. Some are making plans to leave the Episcopal Church.

This is very distressing, but it is easy to understand if one thinks of the legislative process as a war to be won or lost. But the legislative process can be the venue of the Holy Spirit's action within the Church. This is true of the complex formality of a huge ten day General Convention; it is true in the smaller, more familiar deliberations and voting at a diocesan convention such as this, and it is true of the routine decision-making of a parish vestry or outreach committee.

The Risen Christ does not promise easy agreements or simple solutions. Trusting the guidance of the Holy Spirit does not automatically cast out fear of the unknown. It is still hard work, with no guarantees. We were exhausted when we left Philadelphia, and much hard work lies between now and the next Convention.

I earnestly commend the power of civility in the councils of the church—not a facile niceness or politeness or proper manners concealing contempt or hatred, but the civility of the pure in heart who know that we are loved by God despite our sins and simply must share that love with each other. ✠

COUNCIL'S ROLE IN TIMES OF DISSENT
Executive Council, New York City, November 6, 1997

As David Kalvelege pointed out in a recent Living Church editorial, an alphabet-soup of groups have circulated statements expressing unhappiness with decisions made—or not made—at the Convention in Philadelphia. Some appear to be making plans to leave the Episcopal Church. Distressing and confusing as this is, it is a natural and predictable part of our life following every Convention: some Episcopalians are displeased, others are pleased, and responses to the work of the Convention take many forms.

Members of Executive Council often become targets for post-Convention distress and anger, as do the Presiding Bishop or Presiding Bishop-Elect, the President of the House of Deputies, members of the Church Center staff, and anyone else perceived to be part of the mythical "national church." This too is natural, since the General Convention is no longer in session and people want to blame, to appeal to someone to "do something" about whatever has upset them.

It is vital that we listen with respect and compassion to expressions of distress, and respond with accurate information about what the Convention did and did not do. It is also vital that the Presiding Officers and the Executive Council not succumb to the temptation to try to fix things for those who are upset by interpreting away decisions duly made, or suggesting that actions taken in accordance with our Constitution and Canons can be ignored.

We have a pretty ordinary, cut-and-dried way of governing our common life. The Constitution of the Episcopal Church gives authority for decision-making to the General

Convention, made up of bishops and deputies elected by every diocese. Once the Convention is over, those decisions stand until a subsequent Convention changes them. Our system provides an orderly process for such changes, and Episcopal Church history is one long succession of changes affecting liturgy, ministry and social teachings, as we have adapted to meet the needs of proclaiming the Gospel in a continually changing social and cultural milieu.

THE PRESUMPTION OF DIFFERENCE

The whole process presumes that people will have differing views about how and what and when changes ought to be made, and that controversy will sometimes be very intense. Our voting system requires concurrence by both Bishops and Deputies, and, in the case of major questions, a concurrent vote by lay and clerical deputies—which in effect gives each order veto power over the others. This voting system is inherently conservative, promoting stability and preventing precipitous action before a significant level of consensus has developed.

The system does not require total consensus or unanimity before action can be taken, and there is inevitably disappointment among some after each Convention. When those who are disappointed feel strongly about an issue, it's natural for them to question the authority of the body making a decision. But if they appeal to Council to undo something the Convention has done, our obligation is to point them towards the lawful channels for pursuing change in the future, and to remind them of our common responsibility to honor the authorized structures until such time as they may be changed.

This has been true following every General Convention. It has special importance this year because the transition period between one Presiding Bishop's administration and another is a time of ambiguity and uncertainty. It can bring out the worst in us as people jostle for position. New members of Council arrive full of dreams for "fixing" everything their predecessors have messed up, and returning members have similar hopes for a fresh start.

By all means, let us make the most of the dreams and hopes and new ideas that will surface as we become a Council together. But let us also be humble about our place in the total scheme of things. It is not up to Executive Council to fix the Episcopal Church. I'm not at all sure this Church is broken. Our task is rather to BE the Church, elected as servants of all the baptized whose ministries we are called to support, gathered in council as stewards for the triennium of the work of the General Convention.

That's more than enough of a task, and none of us, singly or together, could begin to accomplish it. But with God's help, we need have no fear. ✠

THE RHYTHM OF OUR LIFE
Executive Council, Burlington, Vermont, June 9, 1998

This is the third meeting of the new triennium, and it marks a sort of turning from our focus on follow-up from the previous Convention. Though it's taken a little longer this time because of the transition to a new Presiding Bishop, things are pretty well organized by now for the work we have to do. For the next year or so, we'll do the work, and a year from now we'll be well into the process of deciding how to report on the work to the next Convention.

It's a strange sort of rhythm, not at all like the 3-year lectionary cycle, which gives us different readings but annual observances of the same major feasts. There are no annual observances in the Convention cycle, and I think we are all struck by the way each year itself flies by more quickly than the one before. I guess that's partly a function of age!

But it is also because of the accelerating pace of change in the world all around us and the relentless speed of modern communication. This has definitely affected the way we do business within the Church, and I think it's helpful to reflect on that from time to time.

As leaders of the Church, it is too easy to be distracted by the crises and urgencies of the moment from our baptismal ministries as bearers of the Good News. There's no sure-fire way of avoiding this. Indeed, it often is our responsibility to respond to the crises and the urgencies, and it would be irresponsible not to attend to the deadlines inherent in our 3-year Convention cycle. But we will do better if we remember the larger context of time and place within which we are confronted with decisions about budget planning, appointments, program initiatives, and the myriad other matters that demand our attention. We want to do them well because it will contribute to the life and health of the community, which in turn strengthens our ministry of reconciliation in the world.

That task is an eternal task, in which we are privileged to bear a small part. So let's pray for each other, that we don't get carried away by the pressures of the moment, don't get caught up in feeling indispensable or self-important, as though "saving the Church" or the World depends entirely on us—because of course, God has already done that. All we need to do is bear witness to that hope and promise in our time, as those before us have borne witness in theirs. If we do that, God will take care of the rest. ☥

HOSPITALITY

Diocese of Western Michigan Convention, October 8-9, 1999

I've been thinking about hospitality quite a bit lately, since hearing about the work done by bishops and deputies in Province IV earlier this year. Gathered at the Kanuga Conference Center in North Carolina, under the guidance of a specialist in negotiation, they engaged in what they called "hospitable conversation" in preparation for the 2000 General Convention next summer. Their consultant, Charles Barker, reminded them of the difficulty of remaining open to the spiritual gifts offered by people with whom we have deep disagreements about important things.

In such situations, careful listening in order to understand another point of view is often crowded out by concern to defend ourselves and our point of view. I'm sure you've had that experience when something the other says starts you composing your rebuttal in your head so you don't really hear the rest of what is said.

In a "hospitable conversation" we endeavor to make room for each other, to express our conviction that Christ lives in all of us. This may not be easy, but I suspect that the harder we have to work at it, the greater the blessing. At the Province IV Synod, participants practiced "hospitable conversation" first by discussing matters which unite the church—the baptismal covenant, worship, youth work; and then addressing some dividing issues such as authority and sexuality.

SEEING EACH OTHER AS CHRIST

Trying to stay focused on a call to hospitality, and thinking of how a neutral observer might see a discussion or debate, can help us see and hear the other in a fresh way. We will be more likely to present our best self, balancing rationality and emotion, and to see each other as brothers and sisters in Christ. Then our desire will not be to bully the other into agreement with our clever reasoning or our eloquence, but simply to offer our views and help our conversation partners understand the basis for our position even if they remain opposed to it.

To do this requires great discipline, patience, civility, and respect. Don't be surprised that it often seems very, very hard. Not so long ago in the scheme of things, people chopped off heads and burned each other at the stake as the way to settle conflict. That seems appalling today. However, if you think about the passion and intensity with which we engage some issues, and the verbal violence that sometimes results, we can understand how our ancestors strayed over the line into physical violence in their efforts to preserve "the Faith."

Thank goodness, the Church has changed quite a bit from those days, and change will continue: in organizational structure, in language, in the way we incorporate new members and nurture our children, in our understanding of the mutual ministry of laity and clergy, men and women, in the degree of welcome we extend to those "different" from the "norm," in the way we share our financial resources to support Christ's mission on earth.

We'd be amazed to see the church of the mid-21st century, but the decisions we make now will shape that church of the future. ☦

THE CHURCH AND THE WEDDING GARMENT
Cathedral of the Diocese of Western Michigan, October 10, 1999

Matthew's version of the wedding banquet parable has a dark twist at the end. The king accosts one guest, "Friend, how did you get in here without a wedding robe?" The man was "speechless," and the king ordered him bound and cast into outer darkness.

What is that about? Is it fair to drag everyone in off the streets, and then punish the one who isn't wearing the correct outfit? This parable with its harsh ending may be especially addressed to the Church, to you and me trying to live out ourBaptismal Covenant, trying to respond to God's call to us.

All of us have been called, and the Church is both the community and the institutional framework within which we seek to respond to the call and to extend the invitation to others. What makes the difference between the many and the chosen few? How do we avoid the catastrophic destinies of those who made excuses and wouldn't come, or the one who came without being properly prepared? What is the "wedding robe" we need in order to be prepared, to be the "few" from among the "many"?

Eschew Negativity

Whatever is true...honorable...just...think about these things. It is so easy to get mired in the negative. It's usually the irritations, the problems, the conflicts within our communities that capture our attention. As church leaders it is often our responsibility to deal with these things, to smooth the irritations, to solve the problems, to reconcile the conflicts. We have a duty to face them with courage and intelligence and that usually requires spending at least a little time thinking about them.

But we can only do it safely if we follow the injunction to think even more about what is true, honorable, just, pure. That which is pleasing, commendable, excellent, can be for us a kind of wedding robe. We should immerse ourselves on a regular basis in praise and thanksgiving in our personal prayer and Bible reading, in our weekly Eucharistic celebration, and in our gatherings with other Christians to care for the business side of the church's life—vestry and committee meetings, diocesan conventions, the General Convention.

We need heavy doses of the Good News to inoculate us against the powers of the negative to distract, divide and destroy. We can wrap ourselves in a wedding robe of all those things "worthy of praise" so that we approach our responsibilities for management, decision-making, governance, with a clean heart, with pure motives, with energy whose source is not our own ego-driven needs but the radiant love of God.

I don't want to weep and gnash my teeth in outer darkness, and neither do you. But we can get sucked into controversy to such an extent that we lose our perspective, our bearings, and begin acting as though we're already out there. Some pre-General Convention materials do a lot of weeping and tooth-gnashing.

It's easy to understand. If we don't balance the difficulties that face us with the glorious truths of God's mercy and the brightness of God's love the atmosphere will become murkier and murkier, and we risk finding ourselves outside the closed door—no matter what proposals we champion or positions we espouse. We can't do this by ourselves of course; but we don't have to. God would never call us to something that we—with God's help—could not accomplish.

TIMES OF CONFLICT

Executive Council, San Pedro Sula Cortes, Honduras, October 28, 1999

The history of Christianity is filled with deep conflicts, from the New Testament onward. In some cases they were resolved, but in others they were not, so that today there are a bewildering multitude of Christian bodies, some still openly antagonistic toward others. Within our own Anglican Communion today we have unity-threatening conflicts over the ordination of women, sexuality, and whether lay people can celebrate the Eucharist.

Deep conflicts within the Episcopal Church have led to schisms periodically in the past, and I suppose it will happen again from time to time in the future. We don't like to think about it, and feel an obligation to prevent it; but it does seem to be the case that profound disagreements tend to divide and scatter us. At the same time, there are factors which work against the forces of alienation to draw separated Christians together again, hospitable factors drawing us to care for the stranger, helping us reach across the divides-some of which are very old indeed.

SEASONS OF UNITY

In Harare in December, 1998, the Eighth Assembly of the World Council of Churches began amidst fears of an Orthodox boycott, and the possibility that they might pull out of the Council altogether. The Assembly included many padares (the Shona word for meeting place), forums for education and discussion apart from decision-making or legislation. By the end of the Assembly, both Orthodox and Protestant members had found a new understanding of each others' concerns, a new appreciation and openness to each other and to the Holy Spirit, which led to establishing a three-year "Protestant-Orthodox Dialogue," to explore areas of agreement on which to base common ministry, as well as areas of disagreement which in the past have led to such animosity.

This was an extraordinary development, given a thousand years of separation between the Eastern and the Western Church. It was also clear in Harare that the Roman Catholics, though not yet formal members of the WCC, are increasingly interested in cooperative mission.

Here at home, in our generation, dramatic reunions have taken place and more are under discussion. The ecumenical impulses that led to the founding of both the World Council of Churches and the National Council of Churches half a century ago have contributed to a spreading awareness that the divisions among Christians are a scandal and ways must be found to minimize them.

At a recent meeting of the Standing Commission on Ecumenical Relations, I was impressed once again by the long list of bi-lateral conversations that testifies to our commitment to seek reunion on every side. All these efforts spring from a deep commitment to reconnect the scattered members of Christ's Body. In the midst of them we may feel overwhelmed by the difficulties and discouraged by the seemingly glacial slowness. But step back and look at what God has done with us in just a few decades, after centuries of conflict.

HOSPITALITY, OR A SLIPPERY SLOPE

We are pulled in two opposing directions. On the one side is the call to hospitality, the restoration of broken community by opening ourselves to receive the stranger, who, we are promised, will be Christ for us. On the other side is the slippery slope of distrust, discord and division. It's easy to say which we ought to choose, but it will not be easy to do it.

Already, as the General Convention draws near, the siren calls to preserve right-thinking by rejecting each other are becoming louder. We, as the leaders of the church between now and then—members of Executive Council, together with Deputies and Bishops—must do our utmost to raise the hospitable option again and again, to model openness and welcome for "the other," whatever our perspective or vested interest. We have a grave responsibility, but let's not take ourselves too seriously.

God is with us. The Holy Spirit will inspire us. Jesus Christ has already saved us, and the Church. Good News doesn't get much better than that. ✠

CONVERSION VS. LEGISLATION?

Advent 1999 Letter to Deputies & Alternates

Many people have expressed concern about having time for dialogue among bishops and deputies prior to enacting legislation at the General Convention in Denver in July 2000.

The Presiding Bishop and I, along with other members of the Joint Standing Committee on Planning and Arrangements, are well aware of this concern, and are building into the schedule opportunity for "conversation" on various topics. There will also be hearings on specific topics or resolutions scheduled by legislative committees, at which any member of the Church may share views and raise questions. With this input, committees discuss and decide what recommendations they will offer to the Houses.

Over the past several conventions, we have developed the practice of having the so-called "cognate committees" of the two Houses meet together for most deliberations. Both bishops and deputies work together in the legislative committees on evangelism, on prayer book and liturgy, and so on. Conversations in these meetings acquaint members of one House with the concerns, perspectives and insights of the other, and build important relationships between deputies and bishops. As a result, legislation is well-crafted and more likely to achieve passage in both Houses, and the tension between the two has diminished noticeably.

Some people have suggested that legislation be curtailed at General Convention. Such suggestions recur before each convention, but have become more urgent in recent months. Proponents presumably do not mean we should not vote on a budget to support the various ministries Convention has authorized, or to amend the canons to reflect new ordination practices, or to approve the addition of persons to Lesser Feasts and Fasts. Legislation seems to become suspect, however, when it addresses matters on which a previous consensus no longer exists. For these transitional issues, the prospect of voting raises fears of "losing" on all sides; and when the issue is of great importance, some feel that "losing" will drive them from the church.

THE REAL ISSUE IS....

In our time, the most contentious issues relate to sexuality. In earlier days, sources of major conflict included civil rights, war and peace issues, the use of vestments and candles, slavery, and even whether we should have bishops at all. In each case, the legislative process of our bi-cameral system brought us through profound crisis. Within the legislative framework, guided by the Holy Spirit, sometimes the Convention chooses to move into a new area, sometimes to pull back, and sometimes to take no action at all.

Neither the Presiding Officers nor any other authority can dictate what resolutions bishops, deputies, dioceses and standing commissions may propose or what the Convention will consider. I am confident that the deputies and bishops who come to Denver do so because they love God and the Episcopal Church. No one wants to contribute to schism, nor does anyone want to perpetuate injustice. For at least a dozen years, we have grappled with the challenges of sexuality— in congregational dialogues, diocesan study programs, numerous pre-convention gatherings. At each Convention we have approved some measures, turned down some, and taken no action on others. I expect the Convention will choose a similar path in Denver.

I will continue to encourage opportunities for dialogue and conversation within the daily convention schedule, and I know you will join me in praying for guidance, patience and wisdom as we approach our triennial responsibilities for the governance of the Church. ✠

E-MAIL: A TOOL FOR RECONCILIATION?

Executive Council, New Orleans, Louisianna, January 17, 2000

> *Theologian Konrad Raiser has said that reconciliation is not "a technique that can be learned and applied as a way of peaceful resolution of conflict. It remains a gift of God, and therefore the source of new life." There have been many calls for that gift of reconciliation in the church as General Convention draws near.*

We each prepare for Convention in our own way— praying, studying materials, talking with people in our own dioceses. Now through the miracle of modern telecommunication the majority of deputies and bishops can participate in conversation, exchange of information, testing ideas, sharing views, debating positions via e-mail months before we assemble in Denver. A little bit of this took place before the last convention, but only 19% of deputies had access to it then. As of six months before Convention, that number had almost quadrupled to 72%—with more coming on-line every month. The 2000 Convention will be the first to benefit from the kind of preparation afforded by this non-geographic conversation.

I think this is a good thing. I think e-mail can be an instrument of unity and reconciliation, promoting understanding, reducing the likelihood of misrepresentation that can come from not knowing one another. Human sinfulness being what it is, however, we need to be alert to e-mail's potential—like any other means of communication—to heighten our tendency toward division.

It's not a level playing field yet, and may never be. Though most members of the Convention now have e-mail addresses, some rarely go on-line while others do so several times a day. Using the list gives the illusion of speaking to and hearing from all deputies and bishops, but it's not so. In fact, it would be utterly overwhelming if everyone did participate actively: if the 1000+ members of the two Houses each contributed even a paragraph of comment on each topic, no one would begin to have the time to read them all!

In addition, there is no direct correlation between one's knowledge and wisdom about a topic and one's ability to write about that topic. Nor is the number of words a measure of value. We already know this from our in-person experiences in diocesan councils and conventions—in fact, in just about any setting where many people come together to accomplish a task. But with e-mail we lack facial expression, tone of voice, or the other clues we normally use in interpreting what others say. Maybe a remark which seems very offensive was just meant as a joke. Maybe that long long essay would have been spell-binding as a live speech. We must use this new tool wisely.

Reconciling "Entrenched Bureaucracy" with "Young turks"

Be all that as it may, there have been some lively exchanges on Convention e-mail lists in the past few weeks. The Diocese of Colorado floated a resolution to reduce the size and frequency of the General Convention. I won't comment on the merits of that proposal. However, because these ideas have come up before, I got thinking about the relationship between what feels like cycles of deja vu and the necessary adaptations, changes and developments that characterize the life of any vital organization. Just because an idea came up before doesn't automatically mean we can dismiss it with "been there, done that." On the other hand, those pushing for change do well to learn what the present system is, and why it was set up that way, to avoid coming up with proposals that are redundant or self-defeating.

In the exchanges about the Colorado proposal, there were some none-too-veiled criticisms of the current "leadership" of the church and the General Convention. Once I got past being hurt, I began to wonder how we, as the current leadership, ought to regard the "young Turks" who are full of energy for setting all our errors to right. Most of us were "young Turks" once, and can remember how impatient and judgmental we got about the failure of our elders to see what seemed so obvious to us. Now we're the elders—or the "entrenched bureaucracy," if you will.

We need to listen for the new insights and perspectives of our younger leaders, and offer our own experience and wisdom in a non-combative way. None of us has got everything exactly right. Our task is not to defend—or attack—the "way we've always done it." We must seek instead to reconcile apparently opposing points of view by finding areas of agreement, and then re-framing the conversation on the basis of that unity. ✠

> *The Episcopal Church Women offered programs and a community which provided many women opportunities to develop leadership skills. President Chinnis has always been grateful for this grounding, even as she moved beyond separate women's activities into national and international church service. She never hesitates to name sexism when it rears its head in the church's institutional life, and in speeches has raised the consciousness of many. Her recognition and accomplishments are a source of pride for thousands of women for whom she has opened doors. She doesn't like being a token, but she does it very well indeed.*

Women and the Church

WOMEN AS PIONEERS

Episcopal Church Women, Diocese of Florida, May 14, 1988

As Churchwomen we have a rich history and tradition of women pioneering in the Episcopal Church. We have role models and examples like Marion Kelleran and Cynthia Wedel, two of the all-time great ladies of the Episcopal Church, and many many more. Their efforts paved the way for those of us who followed. Were it not for them, I would not be standing before you today as the first woman elected Vice President of the House of Deputies. I thank them for that.

Role models like these women have had a great influence over women's perceptions of how much we can change our environment, whether it be in the community, the church, or both. Women in the Episcopal Church have always been blessed with vision, but they have also been aware for some time of the major transitions and changes occurring in their lives. Women are now seeking new ways to develop and use their gifts.

These have not been easy years for women, and certainly not for traditional ECW groups. Women have struggled to define their role and their place in a church which has removed the technical barriers to their full participation without removing many of the attitudinal barriers. Some have asked, "Have we gone from auxiliary to invisible?"

Women's history in the Episcopal Church, like all history, is a continuum, so we must look backward as well as forward. Reminisce with me for a few moments. Let your mind wander back 25 years to 1962. What was it like for women in the Church then?

Were there women on the vestry of your parish? Were there women on the Finance Committee? Were there men on the Altar Guild? Were there women acolytes and crucifers? We needn't ask if there were woman priests. There were none. Nor were there any women sitting in the House of Deputies of General Convention, just as there are no women sitting now in the House of Bishops.

MIXED MESSAGES

Why should this be so? In Genesis 1:27 we read, "So God created man in his own image, in the image of God he created him; male and female he created them." Two thousand years ago, through Jesus Christ, women and men were invited into a new covenant with God. "For as many of you were baptized into Christ have put on Christ. There is neither Jew nor Greek, there is neither male no female, for you are all one in Christ Jesus" (Galatians 3:27-28, RSV). However, a funny thing happened on the way to the new relationship.

The Christian Church throughout its history has been deeply influenced by patriarchal traditions and absorbed those traditions into its own life. The role of women and their participation in the church have been influenced by the patterns and customs of society and the patriarchal system that pervades every facet of society. Throughout history, the struggle for emancipation from patriarchy has been uneven. It is sometimes amusing and sometimes irritating that those who fought for emancipation in one area of life were often totally blind to oppression in other areas.

At the Triennial Meeting in 1964, the vision of women like Marion Kelleran and Cynthia Wedel was much in evidence. They were women ahead of their time. Marion made a visionary presentation on Women in Church and Society and Cynthia responded, mentioning the winds of change, the questioning by women of traditional ways, and expressing concern for the wholeness of the Church. And while Cynthia pleaded for "wholeness," the boys over in General Convention applauded the report from the Toronto Anglican Conference on Mutual Responsibility and Interdependence and then voted AGAINST the seating of women in the House of Deputies.

INCHING TOWARD PARITY

With the final seating of women as Deputies two conventions later, in 1970, many thought the millenium had arrived; but as others said, "the timing of inclusion is not important when exclusion is not seen as an injustice—a sin that causes suffering." Even though General Convention had voted to include women they were still largely excluded. Of 88 appointments to interim bodies of General Convention, 50 were clergy (which meant male), 30 were lay men and 8 were lay women. Very few women were elected to anything in 1976; there were only 120 women among 912 deputies, and only 28 women appointed among 200 positions on interim bodies. You get the picture—women were in, but still out. Exclusion was still not seen as a sin.

Women were in a stronger position going into the 1985 Convention. Of 928 deputies, 200 were women—176 lay women and 24 ordained women. Women chaired nine of the 25 legislative committees, and served as vice chair of seven, and of the 200 women deputies, 130 were given committee assignments. Much of the credit for this felicitous state of affairs must go to the then-President of the House of Deputies, Dr. Charles Lawrence, who made all these appointments.

Perhaps it is not so remarkable that it was a black lay man who gave women a chance to prove themselves in the legislative arena. Dr. Lawrence's appointments meant that women not only were given the opportunity to preside over and participate in the important committee sessions where most of the real work was done, but were enabled to be up front, presenting legislation—and presenting it effectively—in the House of Deputies.

Two Steps Forward, One Back

Six lay persons were to be elected to Executive Council at that Convention. Of 12 names proposed by the Nominating Committee, eight were women. A flurry of nominations of lay men from the floor seemed to indicate a concern about the number of women nominated, and when the votes were counted, five men and one woman were elected. When the male power structure in the House of Deputies suddenly realized they were being forced to choose from a slate with more female than male nominees, they successfully blitzed the Convention with additional males, to protect the huge male majority. ☩

WOMEN, MONEY AND THE CHURCH

United Thank Offering 100th Anniversary,
Washington National Cathedral, October 8, 1989

The United Thank Offering (UTO) is a program of the Episcopal Church for the mission of the whole church. It was begun in 1889 by women, and has been administered by women down through the years. The UTO is a way of deepening faith in God through prayer and daily giving. It offers individuals and families the opportunity to show gratitude for the daily blessings of life by encouraging daily prayers of thanksgiving combined with gifts of small coins or bills dropped in a blue box. These individual offerings are united with the gifts of others and used to support new mission work around the world.

The UTO was instituted at a time when women were excluded from the governing boards and decision-making bodies of the Church, yet at the same time they were being encouraged by the decision-makers to raise money for the missionary work of the Church. In 1889, women knew little beyond their own homes, but in every diocese they were recruited to lead others to "work and pray and give" for the extension of Christ's Kingdom. They had limited resources for education—no telephones, radios, movies, TV, no mimeograph machines nor faxes, but they had a sense of urgency and a conviction that God was leading them into being "doers of the Word, and not hearers only."

Women learned very early on that they must be doers of the Word, and the United Thank Offering is symbolic of the truth that the modern mission of our church has been substantially dependent upon its women. Only recently have historians begun to document the history of women's work in the denominations of the church, and the data support the thesis that the religious landscape of mid-nineteenth century America was largely shaped by women and women's organizations within the church.

DOERS OF THE WORD

Women could not officially participate in the national governing body of the Episcopal Church until 1970, and they could not be ordained to the priesthood lawfully until January 1, 1977. Therefore, during the 18th century through well over half the 20th century, women were relegated to a separate, religious "female" sphere. But because women were doers of the Word and not hearers only, they were not content to sit silently in the pew. During the latter half of the 19th century, women took the initiative in inaugurating neighborhood outreach and social-service ministries which became standard features of parish life in the Episcopal Church.

Along with the expansion of parish ministries was the growth of Church-sponsored institutions to serve the community. Almost without exception they were dependent on women volunteers and staff. The move into social-action programs at home was accompanied by the expansion of missionary programs abroad. Women led the way in founding social institutions such as orphanages and homes for the elderly, and in a sense pushed the institutional church into the social gospel. Women recruited, trained, funded and provided pensions for women missionaries abroad. The patterns of social service as a response to the gospel imperative were due in large measure to the work of women in the church, who were peripheral to the centers of power but were "doers of the word and not just hearers."

If women had no official part in the decision-making of the church, how then could they have had such an impact upon the church's mission and its relevance to the social gospel? The answer in large part is due not only to their efforts but to the large amounts of extra-budgetary money they raised, of which the United Thank Offering is undoubtedly the preeminent example in the Episcopal Church. ✠

WOMEN: DREAMERS AND ACHIEVERS
Trinity Church, Piney Branch Rd, Washington, D.C., May 6, 1990

I yearn for the people of the Church to rediscover themselves as the PEOPLE OF GOD. Ministry belongs not to an ordained elite, but to the whole body of believers who are baptized into the love and power of God through Jesus Christ, and who are the *laos*, the People of God. In New Testament times, to say laity or *laos* was to say Christian. The two words were synonymous. The *laos* were those who had been incorporated into Christ through baptism. Through our baptism you and I and all of us have been ordained as members of the royal priesthood. This means that we also have ministerial responsibilities and that we should not hand over the functions of evangelism and pastoral care to certain professional Christians who are paid to perform them.

PEOPLE OF GOD

But how can we reclaim the theological insight that lay people are as responsible to God in their situations and structures and lives as clergy are in theirs? May I suggest three ways we might do so.

Lay people—women and men—must be convinced they do indeed have a ministry within their spheres of primary involvement. In spite of sermons on "the priesthood of all believers" and admonitions to "live your faith in your daily life," too often the structural and liturgical life of the Church continues to reinforce the assumption that there is no valid ministry outside the institutional church. We must affirm that one's work, no matter where or what it is, is holy work because that is the place God has given us an opportunity to serve.

One lay person writing to her bishop said, "I guess my basic frustration is that I can't see anywhere in the Church a recognition of, or much support for, the only kind of ministry that I and most Christians can have—the daily plodding along wherever you are sort of thing, trying to offer up whatever you do to God, rarely seeing how it can make much difference. I've come to think of it as an invisible ministry because it's invisible not only to the church but even to myself most of the time."

RECAPTURING THE AUTHORITY

The root of the problem seems to lie in the assumption that the only valid ministry belongs to the ordained. And lay persons are more often guilty of this assumption than clergy. The story is told of an executive with a major company who is a lay person passionately committed to the ministry of the laity. After a particularly moving talk on her ministry, another layperson said to her, "You should be a minister." When the speaker replied, "I am," her hearer responded, "No, I mean a real minister, an ordained one."

A second way we might nurture lay ministry would be to encourage lay persons to see their job or profession as their "calling" under God. Everyone expects a person preparing for the professional ministry to talk about "a call" and we expect that call to be tested. But we have no similar expectations for lay people, and we believe that lay persons choose their vocation based on personal factors such as skills and interest, salary and opportunities for advancement. If the person is led to believe that she or he chooses a vocation rather than being "called" to a ministry in the world, then we should not be too surprised if lay persons feel that what happens in Church on Sunday has little relevance for what they do with their lives the remainder of the week. When we recognize that all Christian people are called to be ministers and only some of them are ordained, then we will come to appreciate that daily work and divine call are the same and that ministry is the function of the whole people of God.

A third way to strengthen and encourage the ministry of the laity in the world is to recognize that we cannot separate the church and the world. The church should not think of lay people simply in terms of coming in and supporting the church. The more important question for the church to address is how it can support those who are on the front line of the battle, the ones best able to teach the church what Christianity means as a living faith. The world is God's creation and God so loved the world—not the church—that He gave his only begotten Son. The Incarnation means that this secular, worldly life of ours is a fit habitation for the Reality of God. The mundane realm in which men and women drive trucks, run banks, darn socks, teach school and prepare meals is the arena of God's unceasing redemptive activity, and thus the locus of our service to him.

LAY WOMEN IN A PATRIARCHAL INSTITUTION

I have dealt at such length with the ministry of the laity in this sermon on "women dreamers and achievers" because women by and large are the laity. Their dreams and achievements are dictated because they are lay persons, but how they have been permitted and encouraged to exercise their ministries has also been dictated by the fact that they are female in a largely patriarchal institution.

It is paradoxical that an institution such as the Church, which is ordinarily alert to racial prejudice and other social injustices, has seemed so completely unaware of the prejudices operating against women. Indeed, where the Church should be leading the way, we find it often lagging far behind the rest of society. I would love to see the church in the vanguard of pressing for equality of all persons.

In my own involvement with the institutional church, I have seen enormous changes in what women are permitted to do and to be in the Episcopal Church. Historically, most women's activity in the Church has been channeled thorough some kind of separate women's organization. These separate organizations grew up in the 19th century because women were excluded from their denominational governing bodies, and it has been largely through these segregated organizational structures that women have recently been able to move into some positions of leadership and influence within the Church.

It was not until 1970 that women were permitted to be seated as Deputies in the General Convention, and not until 1976 that the ordination of women to the priesthood and episcopate was authorized. Today, in 1990, women as a group—there are individual exceptions—remain observers and supporters rather than decision makers in the Church. The wide range of interests, perceptions and abilities that women have are still denied to the mainstream of the work of the church. For the sake of women, for the sake of men, and above all for the sake of the Church we cannot permit this to continue.

DREAM OF A CHURCH

As women let us dream of a church which develops a greater sense of community—a loving, sustaining community with the powerful presence of the Spirit which transforms the lives of men, women and children.

As women let us dream of a church that makes it possible for people to disagree in love, recognizing that no matter what our differences are, we are brothers and sisters since we are bound together in Christ.

As women let us dream of a shared ministry between clergy and lay people. Let us have more realistic expectations of clergy and their spouses, and recognize that they also need ministering to.

As women let us dream of the full participation of all people—lay and ordained, men and women—in the ministry of the Gospel.

And let us invite our brothers to help us achieve our dreams so that we all may have life and have it more abundantly. ☩

FACING SEXISM
General Convention Sexism Panel, August 26, 1994

Awareness of the problems created by sexism is moving in from the periphery of our corporate consciousness. Eighteen years ago, at the 1976 General Convention in Minneapolis, I was on another panel devoted to sexism—but that was at a small program organized after hours by an unofficial organization, whereas today we are gathered as part of the official Convention program. Then, I was serving as Presiding Officer of the Triennial Meeting of the Women of the Church, while today I am honored to serve as President of the House of Deputies. Then there were about 120 lay women in the almost-900-member House of Deputies, and none in the House of Bishops; today there are nearly 300 lay and clergywomen among the Deputies, and three women in the House of Bishops.

Then we believed that dismantling the legal barriers that kept women out of the governance and ordained ministry of the Church would eliminate inequity and prejudice, and today we can mark significant progress toward that goal. But when I looked back at my notes for that 1976 panel I was struck by how much remains unfulfilled. I said then,

> *As women seek liberation from the restrictions which have limited them to a very narrow range of roles and activities, tension develops—because the basic framework*

of society is still essentially a male-oriented and dominated one. While it is less so now than in the past, the traditional male-oriented societal patterns, customs and thought-forms are still dominant. Sexism runs very deep in our history and culture.

It is less so now—yet still too true, and the tension appears to be escalating, for we have all been profoundly shaped by attitudes so ingrained that rarely do we even see them clearly, much less question them. As the saying goes, "We've come a long way, but still have long way to go."

ANOTHER STEP TOWARD WHOLENESS

Our hope today is to take another step in that journey, to peel away another layer of unconscious assumptions which cripple all of us, men and women, in our relationships with each other, to move closer to the image of God in which male and female are mutually complementary and the Body of Christ stronger and more whole.

We need to do this as a Church for the sake of our own internal health and spiritual integrity. We also need to do it in order to witness boldly to a world in which forms of sexism and misogyny far more blatant than anything Episcopalians might tolerate continue unabated. In some parts of the world infanticide of female babies has reached epic proportions, millions of young women are genitally mutilated, millions here and abroad are kidnapped or sold into a raging sex industry, rape is an official instrument of war, and scarcely a day passes without some horrible story of domestic violence, sexual assault and femicide.

These manifestations of sexism are extreme, yet they are completely consistent with the unconscious conditioning we have all received—women and men alike—conditioning that tracks us into roles and affects not only our view of each other but also our own personal sense of self and the fear we have of one another. This fear—fear of difference, difference of race or ethnicity or gender or sexuality—is profound and insidious, and leads inevitably to hatred and violence unless it is cast out by love. ✠

JESUS, TRADITION AND WOMEN
General Convention Eucharist, August 28, 1994

Jesus was not a scofflaw. He valued the law and the prophets. He knew and valued the traditions of his people. He came not to destroy but to fulfill the law. His approach to law and tradition is crucial for us as we struggle with contradictory understandings of our religious tradition, as we live with "discontinuities" of interpretation and profound conflicts over how God wills us to relate to one another.

What Jesus did was neither to make a god of tradition nor to dismiss it as irrelevant, but to use the whole of tradition as a guide for living in the here and now, seeking beneath the surface of apparent conflicts the core meaning, finding the point of unity between seemingly irreconcilable opposites.

Nothing in our time demonstrates more powerfully the importance of staying with such apparent conflicts as does the emergence of women from the shadows of institutional life to join men in the full life and ministry of the church.

CONFLICT OVER WOMEN'S ROLES

The conflict over women's proper roles has been deep and long-lasting. For most of its life, the Church has consisted of a near-invisible female workforce—tending altars, evangelizing children, nursing the sick, feeding the hungry, caring for orphan and widow—all directed by male clergy and vestrymen. Even the money often came from women, beginning with those who provided for Jesus and his companions out of their own means. Think of them, and of the poor widow whose mite Jesus blessed, as the United

Thank Offering coordinators bring their diocesan offerings forward today.

COMMUNITY RENEWED AND REFRESHED

As women enter the leadership of the church, the life of the whole community is renewed and refreshed. It would not have been conceivable just a few years ago for the General Convention and the Triennial Meeting to gather as we did Friday for a sober exploration of sexism. As the diversity of our leadership expands, our children can grow up with a deeper sense of our mutuality and interdependence within the Body of Christ.

But it does not happen automatically, nor without conflict and pain. Disagreements about women spill over into conflicts about sexuality, as age-old assumptions about human relationships are brought into question. This in turn seems to undermine all our expectations about authority in the household of faith. Many an anguished dialogue, many an angry debate during this Convention turn on just these conflicts.

Jesus' approach to adapting the law in the service of love led him to the cross and grave. Our sins—mine, yours—conspire with the powers of domination and death the way the Pharisees and scribes conspired with Rome. Our sins—yours, mine—join with the spiritual forces of evil to attack and destroy the One who offers freedom and life.

The Good News is that God loves us in spite of these conflicts and our anguished disagreements and our principled opposition and even our nasty attacks on one another. The Good News is that our sins—yours and mine—have been buried in the grave from which Christ rose victorious. The Good News is that God's love overcomes not only your sins and mine, not only the flawed and twisted witness of the Church in the world, not only the broken language in which we try to tell others that we have seen the risen Christ, but all the principalities and powers of falsehood, and domination, and even death itself.

That is the Good News that enables us to continue on our journey despite conflict and confusion and darkness. That is the Good News, whether we can comprehend it or not. For as God assured Julian of Norwich, "All shall be well, and all shall be well, and all manner of things shall be well." ☩

WOMEN'S HIDDEN WORK
Church Club of New York, February 22, 1995

Until very recently, women's life in the church has been hidden, almost invisible. Episcopal women, perhaps more than most, have tended to live out the ideals of womanly behavior dominant in the larger society. For centuries this has meant embracing a secondary role in the family, in the community, and in the church. A good woman was one who supported her husband through thick and thin (even if he mistreated her or the children), raised those children to be industrious, law-abiding citizens, and kept the local church going through dedicated service on the altar guild, as Sunday school teacher, in the parish kitchen, or raising money from Christmas ornaments made out of old detergent bottles.

I don't mean to put down any of those activities (except maybe tolerating an abusive spouse). I've done most of them myself, and received a lot of satisfaction from the sense of service and the companionship which have always been inherent in "women's work." But I thank God that I live in a time when barriers preventing women from doing anything else in the church are falling. Had I come to a Church Club annual meeting as a young woman, I would have been permitted to sit in the balcony with other wives to listen to the speech while the men mingled freely for dinner and conversation. I'm awfully glad—and I expect you all are too—that tonight we can eat and talk together. But I suspect we all also share a slight embarrassment that this is still a new enough phenomenon to be worth talking about.

So what did it used to be like, and why is it changing?

Conjure up an image of what the church was like a century or two ago. In the foreground, lots of men in dark suits gathering earnestly to do the church's business, and occasionally, in the background, glimpses of women—in silk or homespun, voluminous country shifts or cinch-waisted bustles—herding children, tending the sick, serving food, polishing candlesticks.

That's the image preserved and passed along to us in our parish records and diocesan archives and—until very recently—in the official accounts and scholarly histories written about the Episcopal Church. In terms of the "public" face of the church, it is a reasonably accurate image. Clergymen and vestrymen had charge of the worship and governance of local parishes and dioceses, male bishops and deputies constituted the General Convention. The standard history of the Episcopal Church used by seminarians until very recently mentions over four hundred men, but only thirteen Episcopal women, most of them wives or mothers of bishops, plus six queens of England![1] Most diocesan and parish histories merely chronicle the clergy and buildings, because that is what was preserved in the record. Now we are discovering what a pale, one-dimensional image that male-only picture of church life has always been.

NEW PATTERNS OF RELATIONSHIP

Although God's love is everlasting, the world in which we experience it is full of change. In our time, that change is perhaps most profound in terms of the intimate relationships

---

[1] James Thayer Addison, The Episcopal Church in the United States, 1789-1931 [NY: Charles Scribner's Sons, 1951]

between men and women, and all the other social structures that flow from that pattern.

As unsettling as that is, it is also cause for great thanksgiving and hope. Men and women are able to deal with the daily requirements of life, and with the challenges of a new age, far more effectively as partners than when locked into single-sex roles. We have an opportunity to develop truly new approaches to social problems and to religious issues, to personal relationships and to organizational structures.

Since my election as President of the House of Deputies in 1991, I have been blessed by an ever-deepening collaboration with the Presiding Bishop as we exercise our responsibilities in the Church. The pattern of shared leadership that we are discovering is a symbol for me of the possibilities for all Christian men and women as we learn to work together as equal partners. After all, as Genesis suggests, to produce an image of God in human form required the creation of both male and female. Alienated, we are both casualties of the war between the sexes; but together we can become a powerful voice to proclaim the Good News of Jesus Christ to our troubled world. ☩

CHANGING ROLE OF
WOMEN'S ORGANIZATIONS

Episcopal Church Women
Diocese of Long Island, New York, May 10, 1997

The movement toward greater cooperation and collaboration, and away from hierarchical structures, is one of the healthy products of the changing place of women in the Church today. We are no longer strictly segregated in women's organizations. Since 1970, the Episcopal Church has welcomed women to the House of Deputies and to the ordained ministry. In 1988 we elected our first woman bishop, and in 1991 I was privileged to become the first woman elected president of the House of Deputies.

The Woman's Auxiliary and the Episcopal Church Women were the training ground for these developments. The first women to serve on the Executive Council and as Deputies had been leaders in the Woman's Auxiliary, and the first presidential gavels I wielded were those of the ECW in my home diocese of Washington DC, and that of Presiding Officer of the 1976 Triennial Meeting.

These very visible developments symbolize increasing mutuality in the participation of both men and women in the Episcopal Church. We are steadily living into the commitments of the Baptismal Covenant, which call each of us to active involvement in the worship and ministry of the Body of Christ. This takes different forms in different areas, reflecting the increasing cultural diversity of both the church and the society. The ECW itself has evolved as the patterns of women's lives have changed at home and in the workplace.

DIFFICULT ADJUSTMENTS

Sometimes that may seem a bit chaotic, and it can lead to conflict. In some places, ECW chapters and altar guilds languish for lack of younger recruits. Some have changed their names in search of new constituencies. Some dioceses have gone so far as to abolish the ECW, and have often found that more than half the energy and networking ability to get things done in the diocese went along with it.

Vestries upset by the independence of the ECW sometimes try to co-opt traditional "women's work" into parish-wide study groups and fund-raising committees. Clergy are sometimes offended by the so-called "liberal" work of many ECW groups, and instead promote what they think of as the more "conservative" Daughters of the King. If they think women who pray will be less troublesome, they're in for some surprises!

Such problems are "growing pains"—the kind of adjustments and adaptations that naturally accompany our growth into being fully the Body of Christ, made in God's image— male and female.

This makes our generation a particularly challenging and wonderful time to be alive. God has called us to worship and service at a wonderful transition point in the life of the Church. ✠

MOTHERLY ADVICE

Celebration of Southern Episcopal Church Women
Kanuga Conference Center, Hendersonville, North Carolina,
June 6, 1998

Let me sound a practical, motherly-advice note, since there has to be something besides arthritis that accompanies aging—the freedom to offer advice!

Don't forget your history and those who made it possible for you to attain what you have. Remember other women have laid the groundwork for what becomes possible in each new period. During the election process in the Diocese of Washington at the time Jane Dixon became our suffragan, there were some clergy women who spoke disparagingly about the activities of the "old-time" lay women. That hurt, a lot. Had it not been for those old lay women, those clergy women might not yet have been wearing their collars.

If you want to serve in the decision-making councils of the Church, be willing to start at the bottom. Learn the system, and be willing to do the nitty-gritty jobs. Just do them better than anyone else! Cultivate your power base—and remember that "power" is not a bad word. The institutional church is, among many things, a political system—and "politics" is not a bad word either, though the way some politicians conduct themselves often discredits the whole enterprise. To me, politics is about how we negotiate the balance of power within the system, in order to direct our corporate energy to achieve the common good. Viewed this way, "politics" is a good thing, and we need to be smart about how we participate.

So long as men still dominate the Church—and make no mistake about it, they do—like it or not women will often have to depend on men to help them enter the system. And once given the opportunity, they will have to prove themselves in ways men are never expected to do. If you are "the first" at anything, there is added pressure to outperform everybody else simply because you are the first. So be sure to do your homework. One can't "wing it" for very long.

Help other women along the way. Don't fall prey to the Queen Bee Syndrome, holding power to yourself and blocking the path of others. Don't become a closet matriarch.

LEARN TO MAKE WAVES

I urge for you a commitment to personal growth. As a woman raised not to make waves, I can tell you how painful it is to grow beyond the narrow confines of traditional roles. I can also tell you how rewarding it is to expand your interests, broaden your tastes, activate your sense of fair play and justice, learn to make sacrifices and to love more fully.

Take nothing for granted. Question every direction, every course of action you take. Root out the assumptions you live with simply because they have been old friends over the years, and subject them to the harsh light of scrutiny. Don't be afraid to speak up when you have something to say.

Please develop your sense of humor. Without it your life will quickly go stale. With it, you can be gentler on your own personal shortcomings, and on the idiosyncrasies of others. Your sense of humor and your perception of the comic in a situation will preserve you from many moments of hysteria, ill-will and bad-naturedness.

Finally, how much does a woman's personal leadership style have to do with breaking down the barriers and opening the door for other women in the future? Carol Becker, in her 1996 book *Leading Women: How Church Women can Avoid Leadership Traps and Negotiate the Gender Maze,* notes that as women have entered church leadership in significant numbers, the acceptable styles of leadership have multiplied. I come from a background that permits me not to have to be defensive about nor confrontational in my leadership style. There are those who feel and act differently, and I respect those differences and recognize there is room for a great diversity of gifts and ministries in this world.

COMPROMISE WHAT COMES "NATURALLY"

However, as Becker also notes, women in leadership must be prepared to compromise what comes "naturally" because the church remains fundamentally a male hierarchy. Theology and language continue to work against us, and patriarchal notions of the supremacy of the male make sexism appear normative even to ourselves. Women need mentoring, from men who can show them how to survive in a male-centered culture, and from other women who can help them stay true to their own style even in an unfriendly environment.

However we do it, the ministry of all of us is about shedding the pressures of oppression, whether it be sex, race, or class, freeing men as well as women of the pressures of oppression so that all can be reconciled to one another and to God through Christ.

This is a high calling—the highest calling of all, to which all are bound by the covenant of Baptism, through which we become the daughters and the sons of God. That's what this girl from the Ozarks has learned from a long and often amazing journey. Thank you for letting me share it with you. ✠

150TH ANNIVERSARY, 1ST WOMEN'S RIGHTS CONVENTION

Dedication of Robert Lenz Icon of Elizabeth Cady Stanton
Trinity Episcopal Church, Seneca Falls, New York, July 19, 1998

I hope that Elizabeth Cady Stanton and the companions who joined her in the Wesleyan Chapel one hundred and fifty years ago today were able to hold fast to the promise contained in today's Gospel reading: "Because of your persistence, the friend will get up and give whatever is needed. So I say to you, Ask, and it will be given you; search, and you will find; knock, and the door will be opened." Luke 11: 8-9 (Oxford, *New Testament: An Inclusive Version*, 1995).

They must have believed it at the start. How else could they have had the courage or energy to begin such a long struggle, to challenge the status quo, to ask for the unthinkable: equal rights for women, universal suffrage, an end to discrimination? They must have believed it as the months turned to years, and the years became decades. How else would they have had the strength to continue?

PERSISTENCE AND PERSPECTIVE

From our perspective, in a world so utterly different now from theirs—different in part because of their long labors — what Stanton and her companions began just down the street from here appears noble, far-sighted, the launching of a great movement destined for success, though their neighbors probably thought they were idealistic cranks or trouble-makers, or wicked opponents of the God-given order of the world, or silly women....

From our perspective, the seventy-two-year struggle from that day until the Nineteenth Amendment authorized women's suffrage appears telescoped through the lens of success. The ridicule and opposition and set-backs are framed by victory. We see a steady progress through American history to an inevitable moment of triumph.

And perhaps, in those first heady days, Stanton and company had a glimpse of the end, too, felt its inevitability in their hearts, "knew" that they would succeed because the truth was so self-evident.

We know that suffrage was eventually achieved, and that women's lot is radically different today than it was when they began. They didn't live to see the success we take for granted now: Mott died in 1880, Truth in 1883, Bloomer in 1894, Stanton in 1902, Anthony in 1906, Tubman in 1913. These were flesh and blood women who lived and died in the hope of something better; colorful, quirky women, flawed but inspiring, scared but powerful, willing to take enormous risks and able to endure humiliation, scorn, contempt, derision, because they had a glimpse into a different way of being in the world and could no longer live content with the way things were.

Proclaim a Different Vision

This glimpse into a "better way," and the power it gave them to stand up against overwhelming odds, is really what today's Scripture readings are all about. They speak to our need to understand what enables people to step out of their "proper place," to defy the authorities of their day and proclaim a different vision, to persevere as prophets who—we are told elsewhere—are never honored in their own country.

> *"In every generation Wisdom passes into holy souls and makes them friends of God and prophets." (Wisdom 7:28) It is Almighty God "who gives justice to those who are oppressed, ...sets the prisoners free, ...lifts up those who are bowed down."* (Psalm 146:7-8)

Being a prophet is hard work, long and lonely work, holy work. Our notions about separation of Church and State notwithstanding, religion and politics have always been inextricably bound together in American history. And so they should be, for politics is the working out in practice of our conviction about how people should behave toward one another, which is always ultimately a religious question. Stanton and her companions in the reform movements of the 19th century—abolitionists, suffragettes, urban reformers, temperance leaders—were unabashedly motivated by religious principles and inspired by personal faith.

Because their convictions about God's will for the world led them to challenge the status quo, they were often—like Jesus—at odds with religious authorities as well as the secular powers-that-be. Like many who struggle against patriarchy today, they were often estranged from the patriarchal church. But that shouldn't confuse us about the source of their strength.

In their day, as in our own, many who feel most inspired by God to work on behalf of the suffering and oppressed become estranged from the very religious institutions which first offered them the Good News of Jesus Christ. The story is told about Elizabeth Cady Stanton, that as a youngster she belonged to a girls club at church which took on the support of a young seminarian as a project. The girls sewed and baked to raise money for this man's studies. When he graduated, they gave him a new black suit, silk hat and cane, and eagerly attended when he came to preach in their congregation. He chose as his text I Timothy, 2:21: "But I suffer not a woman to teach, nor to usurp authority of the man, but to be in silence." Stanton and the other girls, the story goes, rose and left the church in silent protest.[2]

---

[2] As told by Jeanne Stevenson-Moessner, "Elizabeth Cady Stanton, Reformer to Revolutionary: A Theological Trajectory," Journal of the American Academy of Religion, LXII/3, p.673.

EARLY CONSCIOUSNESS-RAISING

Obviously her consciousness was raised even then, and she was frequently to charge that the power of the clergy was a key element in the subordination of women. Stanton was not afraid to assign responsibility for what today we call "institutional sexism" in the Church, using that strong clear language which was her hallmark: "These things were not done by savages and pagans, they were done by the Christian Church!"[3]

Those of us involved in changing women's roles in the Episcopal Church in the final third of the twentieth century can relate easily to Stanton's 19th century outrage. It was not until 1970, fifty years after the Suffrage amendment to the US Constitution, that women could vote in the General Convention of our Church, and there are still places where women's ordination is vehemently opposed.

But we can take inspiration and strength from the propers for today's celebration. The Gospel promises that we will be given all that we need, if we are persistent, if we keep faith, if we do not lose hope. The Gospel promises that our God is the God who wants to give good gifts to every one of us, and that one of those gifts will be God's own Spirit—that Wisdom which "passes into holy souls and makes them friends of God and prophets."

Like Elizabeth Cady Stanton and her companions, we too are called by God in our time to complete the work set in motion at Creation, to set to rights things that have been subverted, to bring justice to the oppressed and food to the hungry, and to lift up those who are bowed down.

The Spirit of God guides us into all truth and makes us free, and will give us vision and courage just as they were

---

[3] Text on the scroll of the icon of Elizabeth Cady Stanton, by Robert Lentz, commissioned for Trinity Church, Seneca Falls, NY.

given vision and courage. We also will be empowered to stand against oppression and injustice in our day as they stood in theirs. Let us thank God for the example of Elizabeth Cady Stanton, and of all the strong and courageous women who have gone before us, and trust God's grace that we may follow in their footsteps. Like them, we are called to take our places in the great sweep of salvation history moving toward that glorious liberty which God has prepared for all of us through the life and death and resurrection of Jesus Christ. ✠

LOOKING BACK, LOOKING FORWARD

Women at General Celebration,
General Theological Seminary, April 19, 1999

Women at seminary, theologically-educated laywomen, women as deacons and priests and bishops—what does all this mean for the Church?

There are plenty of Episcopalians now who have no experience or memory of the Church before it was the norm for women to go to seminary, or to be ordained. Lucky for them, and yet there is a danger. Open access for women to leadership positions on the same basis as men is by no means universal, or guaranteed. We should never take it for granted. Still, each year's seminary graduating classes, each year's round of ordinations, helps to improve the balance not just for women but for the whole Church.

So long as theological education, whether leading to ordination or to some other form of professional ministry, was the sole province of men, the Church expressed and perpetuated a sadly distorted theology, which overemphasized maleness in beliefs about God and the proper ordering of the human and ecclesial communities. This distortion rendered women and girls invisible in the texts and worship and decision-making of the Church.

All this is changing now, gradually, painful step by painful step, as theologically-trained women spread slowly throughout the Church and move into more and more positions of leadership.

EDUCATION IS KEY

Theological education is the essential key to being taken seriously within the Church's ministry structures, and all our seminaries have dropped their exclusive policies and struggle to learn what "coeducation" might mean in a seminary context. Let me repeat here that I am not just talking about seminary as preparation for ordination. Many lay women, with no call to ordination, have studied here and in other seminaries. Some move into program responsibilities in parishes, dioceses or national ministries. Many pursue vocations in education, from Sunday school to graduate level teaching, some even in seminaries.

Well before the 20th century even began, women sought education and training for a wide variety of ministries within the church. First at the deaconess training schools, and then for many decades at St Margaret's House in Berkeley, California, and Windham House in New York City, women found ways to circumvent the male-only restrictions on theological education.

Let me assert now my firm belief that it was the several generations of Windham House and St Margaret's House graduates who paved the way for the admission of women to the House of Deputies, and to the ordained ministries of this Church. Against tremendous odds, they demonstrated that women's mysterious brains could handle New Testament Greek and that their delicate constitutions would not be overwhelmed by the rigors of church history or systematic theology.

"WOMEN CHURCH WORKERS"
PAVE THE WAY

When they went forth to serve the Church, especially the generation who staffed the burgeoning Christian Education programs of the 1950s and 60s, they infiltrated diocese after diocese with examples of intelligent, articulate, theologically-educated women (often sharper than the ordained men they worked for!). There is no doubt in my mind that their presence as professional ministers in a variety of settings had a tremendous influence on the discussions and debates which led to the removal of the exclusion of women from church governance and from the ordained ministry.

Some of them may have longed for ordination themselves (and some were ordained when it became possible), while many others felt secure in their lay vocations. Many lay women worked politically for the ordination of women, not because they wanted to be ordained themselves but because they wanted their lay ministries to be a choice among alternatives, not the only course open to them.

As in so many areas of life, education was a critical element in changing the dynamic, opening doors which had been closed. Women in seminary, seminary-educated women in the Church—there is no question that their cumulative influence has dramatically re-shaped the Episcopal Church in the twentieth century. Thank God for that! ☩

Do Justice

He has told you, O mortal, what is good;
and what does the Lord require of you,
but to do justice, and to love kindness,
and to walk humbly with your God.
                              —Micah 6:8

Confronting Racism in a Changing Church

Episcopal Urban Caucus, February 25, 1994

I hardly need tell you that the church and society are both in a time of critical change and it will no longer be possible to do business as usual. What does this mean for our Church and society as we attempt to confront our own personal and institutional racism in the waning years of the 20th century? What are the trends for the future that will have an impact on all we do?

We have moved from a church in a self-confident society to being a church in a fearful society. Change is crowding in on us at an ever-accelerating rate. Edwin Friedman has observed that the capacity of a community to cope is in inverse proportion to the anxiety level. If we are a fearful society, what impact will that have on our relations with one another? Do we become more ingrown, more suspicious, less tolerant than those different from us?

We have gone from a church of affluence to one with shrinking resources. What does that mean for national Church structures and for churches doing ministry on the local level? We have had to cut back on aid to the historic Black colleges, to APSO, AIDS, and on and on. Will local congregations have the vision and the resources to pick up those programs that fall through the cracks?

We are moving from church-wide planning to local initiatives. What help do we need in doing this? More money is staying on the local level, but local planners are going to need assistance in planning and networking. We are moving from an emphasis on "professional" Christians—meaning clergy— to Christian professionals—meaning laity. But in the transition period there are many rough patches.

We are moving from hierarchical models of church leadership to participatory models. People want a voice in what affects them. Can you blame them? At a recent Province VIII Synod, there was to be a panel on the Church in the future. All three panelists were white Anglo-Saxons, although Province VIII is probably one of the most culturally diverse provinces in the Episcopal Church. There was a loving but adamant demand that the panel be expanded to include ethnic minorities represented in the Synod. It was done, and the result was incredibly rich. We—or I should say, the dominant culture—can be so amazingly obtuse at times.

TOWARD AN ANTI-RACIST SPIRITUALITY

There is less obsession with individualism and more emphasis on solidarity. We are beginning to realize that we are all in this together for the long haul, and privatized religion isn't the way to go any longer. It seems to me that I have even detected less reluctance to pass the Peace than there once was. We are moving from a single culture to a multicultural community of faith. The melting pot hasn't melted. Some have suggested it is a salad bowl. In a preface to

"Ministry in a Culturally Diverse Church," Presiding Bishop Browning wrote, "The imperatives of the gospel challenge us to minister in the place and time we are right now. This means we are called to minister in a multicultural and multiethnic society." Most of us in leadership positions really don't know how to do this very well.

When the Presiding Bishop and I made appointments to Interim Bodies after the 1991 General Convention, we were both committed to making them as inclusive as possible. I think we both were pleased that we had made some progress, but as the old ad suggests, "We've still got a long way to go." I need your help on this—to keep me honest and to call me to account, and to tell me who the qualified people are. And we know it is not enough simply to make appointments at the national level. There must be a "trickle down" effect in provinces, dioceses and parishes. Can we discover a way to have authentic pluralism and authentic community, and not just a superficial façade?

What can we do to work toward a spirituality of anti-racism? We have to begin where we are. We must confront racism and it must begin with us. We must remember that our comfort level is not the driving force in our actions. We must do what is hard and painful. ✠

SEEKING UNITY

Episcopal Church Women,
Diocese of Southeast Florida, May 12, 1995

We seek unity because on the night before he died Jesus Christ himself prayed fervently that God would give us unity; Jesus shared his resurrection "glory," given him by the Father as a sign of their oneness, in order that we too might be one, so that the whole world would know that Jesus came as a sign of God's utterly boundless love for all humankind.

Our unity is to be a sign of God's love for all humanity.

Our unity is to be a sign of God's union with Christ Jesus, the incarnation of the divine in human form. Our unity is to be a sign that no one is beyond the reach of God's love.

This universal aspect of the Gospel message makes our celebration of diversity not just a nice open-minded thing to do, not just a tolerant attitude or a political stance, not just a fuzzy, "y'all come" sort of generic welcome. We celebrate diversity NOT to be open-minded but because God's universal love demands that we do.

Only to the extent that we, as Christians and as the Church, are able to love one another across the lines of our differences—to rejoice with all our hearts that we are not all the same, to recognize that without every single one of us humanity would be incomplete and God's creative design would be frustrated, to feel in the depths of our being how each of us contributes a unique aspect to the full glory of all that God has made—only to that extent can the world around us know the Good News of Jesus Christ, that God sent him, and loved him, and loves us beyond all weakness and sin and death and the grave, that God longs for all of us to return to Zion with singing, to walk through blooming deserts and drink from cool springs, to open the eyes of the blind and heal the sick and even to raise up the dead as Christ was raised for us all.

No Unity Without Diversity

This is the amazing thing: there can be no true unity without diversity. Sameness is not unity. The warm feelings I have when I gather with like-minded people are not unity. The comfortable meetings where we all know the rules and agree on our goals and how to accomplish them are not unity.

The voluntary gatherings of those who share the same tastes or beliefs—the same color or ethnic heritage, the same age or sexuality, the same work or play or preferred forms of worship—those voluntary gatherings can be essential to provide experiences of safety and acceptance, models of identity, celebration and thanksgiving for our unique gifts, but they are not unity.

Only when we bring together those separate experiences of our differences—with all the friction and confusion that produces, the loss of neatness and control, the disorientation of not knowing all the "rules," the discomfort of not being able to anticipate how people will respond because they're are not the same as I am—only as we are able to live with that uncomfortableness, to let go of our fear of people we don't understand, to learn to listen first and to look through the eyes of others, only as we let the glory of God in Christ Jesus truly transform our lives together, only then can we begin to live in the Unity for which we pray. ☥

PREPARING TO STRIVE FOR JUSTICE

Justice Summit, Cincinnati, Ohio, February 27, 1997

We have come to this Justice Summit because we share a common Baptism, and with it the imperatives of the Baptismal Covenant:

- continue in the apostles' teaching, the Eucharistic fellowship and prayer;
- resist evil and repent when we fall into sin;
- proclaim by word and example the Good News of God in Christ;
- seek and serve Christ in all persons, loving our neighbors as ourselves;
- strive for justice and peace among all people, respecting the dignity of everyone human being.

These shared baptismal commitments can be a powerful force for good, and I am enthusiastic about the energy, and the synergy, that has developed here.

We celebrate our common concerns for justice as we gather them together here. I hope that we emerge from this Summit with an affirmation of all the concerns we share this weekend. Our time together is not about deciding that some issues are more important than others. Rather it is about identifying common concerns, seeing how they relate to the fundamental issues of justice, and developing a strategy or strategies for the church's future prophetic witness.

This is an opportunity to share our various concerns and develop a sense of direction for the justice ministries of this Church as we move forward into a new era. It is time for us to take stock, to build connections, to renew our faith and love and commitment, to celebrate the Good News of Jesus Christ in our day as countless hosts have done before us.

So work hard, listen hard, think hard, pray hard. Above all, let the Holy Spirit move among us, that we may be instruments of God's will in a world hungering for peace and justice. ✠

REMEMBERING ABSALOM JONES

African Episcopal Church of Saint Thomas,
Philadelphia, Pennsylvania, July 20, 1997

Let us remember those now forgotten, who lived and died and left nothing more behind them than an entry in a ledger, or on a bill of sale.

Let us remember a time in this country when some human beings were owned by other human beings. This was a time when slavery was not just a phenomenon in the Southern states, but in Northern states as well. This was a time when statesmen and presidents—and arguably the finest president this country has ever had—were themselves both the architects of freedom and the owners of slaves.

Let us remember the day even before the freedom of this country from Britain—30 years before the Declaration of

Independence, on 6 November 1746 in fact—when a particular slave was born in Sussex County, Delaware. Absalom Jones, that young slave, grew into a life of toil—the toil of work, and the toil of teaching himself to read by poring over the New Testament.

Let us remember the circumstances which conspired to bring him to Philadelphia. Here Absalom Jones was able to earn money of his own "after hours," to attend a night school for blacks run by Quakers, to buy his wife's freedom and later his own, to purchase a house and build two others to earn additional income. What uncommon ability all of this must have taken.

Let us also remember all the educated, free African Americans who were beginning to take their destiny into their own hands. When Absalom Jones and his friend Richard Allen, along with many others, refused to be segregated in the gallery of Saint George's Methodist Episcopal Church in 1787, they set a trend which was to be followed by their brothers and sisters in churches up and down the East Coast. For them, refusing to sit in the gallery of a church was like the refusal of their descendants to sit at the back of a bus.

The Free African Society which Jones and Allen formed gave birth to a congregation called "The African Church" in 1792, the first organized congregation for African Americans of any denomination in this country. Bishop William White ordained Absalom Jones to the diaconate in 1795, and to the priesthood seven years later, making him the first black priest of this Church and the first black ordained by any church in this country.

THE LONG SEARCH FOR FREEDOM

For 23 years Absalom Jones served this congregation, and it grew remarkably under his leadership. But not all was easy. As we remember the success, let us remember also the heartache and failure. There was that great parting of friends, when

Richard Allen left the Free African Society and went on to form the African Methodist Episcopal Church. There was the difficulty of incorporating the parish into the Diocese of Pennsylvania, and the shameful device used for its exclusion: the fact that Absalom Jones had no Latin or Greek was used as a reason to deny the African Episcopal Church of Saint Thomas full participation in the Diocesan Convention. We could clear the halls and shorten the business at General Convention considerably if we imposed the same rules on ourselves today!

We must always remember, when we are tempted to think that racism in our nation is the characteristic of an odd, misguided minority, who live somewhere else. We must always remember, when we are quick to criticize other nations for sins the practice of which we are still guilty. We must always remember, when we fall into the temptation that we can address the rift of racism in our society by tightening up immigration laws or by building higher, more effective fences. If we have learned anything from the history of civilization, whether in ancient China, or in Roman Britain, or in modern Europe, it is that no wall, whether to keep human beings in, or to keep them out, can resist the unconquerable spirit of the human heart to be free.

The freedom of the Gospel is not the easy rest of indifference; it is the chains of love and commitment. We do all this so badly in the Church sometimes. But that is no excuse for not trying to do better. For the freedom of the Gospel is the truth that, by God's grace, we can do better if we try. As Saint Paul expressed so eloquently in the second Letter to the Corinthians, the Church's "power is made perfect in weakness." ✠

RESPONSE TO THE NEW
JAMESTOWN COVENANT

Jamestown, Virginia, November 1, 1997

It is a very difficult thing to stand here today as representative of an institution which participated in the oppression of native peoples on this continent. It would be so much easier to slither out of responsibility. I might protest: "I wasn't there, none of us were there, then, when terrible things were done by invaders in the name of God and country, civilization and Christianity."

I could cite the classic defense: that my predecessors didn't know any better; they were doing the best they could, as they understood the world and the Gospel; that they sincerely believed and intended their actions to be for the good of those they encountered. I could say those things, and they all would be true, but you and I would know that they are irrelevant. Good intentions do not excuse evil deeds. The Church of today must own up to the sins of yesterday.

We must repent on behalf of those who went before us, shedding the tears of remorse they would shed if they saw their actions from our perspective. Most of all, the Church of today must not let shame and guilt from the past prevent us from fulfilling our responsibilities in the present.

CALLED TO ACTION

The new Jamestown Covenant summons us to action for the future. It calls us to continue the process of remembering, seeking reconciliation within the context of learning more and more about who we have been with and toward each other. Unless we know our history, we are doomed to repeat its mistakes.

The Covenant calls us also to renewed social and political effort. Thousands upon thousands still suffer the consequences of centuries of abuse, hostility and neglect. We who live today did not create the original situation; but judgment shall rest harshly upon us if we fail to address the results in our own time.

The Covenant challenges us to find new ways to speak across the great divide between native traditions and the form of English Christianity evolving on these shores. This means celebrating the richness of each heritage. It also means recognizing that powerful symbols may carry conflicting meanings within different cultural contexts. We are constantly at risk of offending—or simply baffling—each other. So we must pray together earnestly for the peace and unity that comes from God alone.

Finally, the Covenant commits us to care for the Earth as our home, as a sacred trust from the Creator. In the long sad tale of expansion across this continent, lack of respect for the environment has gone hand in hand with lack of respect for each other. This deadly approach must be abandoned. Our own health and that of generations to come depends upon it. Indeed, if we fail in this trust, there may be no generations to come. So we commit to honoring the Earth as God's creation, and each other as the people of God.

What we do here today marks another stage in the maturing of the Episcopal Church's understanding of its responsibilities to its Native American members. It does not "fix" the past, but it signals a present commitment to work for a different future, for ourselves and for all of our children.

May God have mercy on us, and uphold us in sharing the good news of what we do here today, that all those whom we represent may know the blessings of a new beginning, share in ever-richer fellowship one with another, and recognize the power of the Holy Spirit drawing us deeper into God in Christ Jesus. ✠

AN AGE OF CYNICISM AND APATHY?
Executive Council, Fond du Lac, Wisconsin, June 14, 1999

At this Spring's Charter Day at the College of William and Mary, Timothy J. Sullivan, President of the College, reflected at some length on the perils facing our country in an age of cynicism and apathy. His remarks were chiefly in response to the public crisis related to the impeachment trial, but they apply easily to the Church as well.

What has "degraded our public life and fueled public cynicism?" Sullivan asks. He considers the most potent force to be "a stunning popular ignorance about our constitutional system and the defining events in our national history."

Substitute "American church history" for "national history" and the message is the same: from ignorance flows lack of interest or involvement, breaking the connection of trust and accountability that must exist between leaders and those they represent in society, and in the church.

President Sullivan's observations were, perhaps, expressed in especially pessimistic terms because they came right on the heels of President Clinton's trial in the Senate. But his analysis of the ills besetting the body politic—the church politic—is nonetheless painfully accurate.

Despite being impressed, even inspired, by the enthusiasm for mission and outreach of so many people "in the pews," I have also been dismayed by their lack of knowledge about the most basic facts of Episcopal Church history and governance. How can Episcopalians provide guidance to their leaders or understand the implications of decisions made if they don't know the institutional and historical framework along with the biblical and theological foundations?

"Majority" vs. "Minority" Interests

Here is another passage from Sullivan's address which I found especially helpful to understanding one aspect of life in the church today:

> *A public culture crippled by apathy and infected by ignorance spawns other enemies of freedom. As more and more reject the idea of active citizenship, many who remain engaged embrace intensely focused but narrow views. These activists are passionate about a single issue and indifferent to all others. They are one-cause citizens, and they see the complexities of our time through the distorting prism of a glass that makes balance impossible and context irrelevant. Name the subject, you will find a 'one-cause caucus' eager to impose what are inevitably minority views upon an indifferent, and thus underrepresented, majority.*[1]

The parallels with our experience are obvious. I would like to suggest, however, that we in the Church have an opportunity to develop and model for the world another way of dealing with "one-cause" forces, a way that moves beyond the anxiety and frustration they so often elicit.

I suspect President Sullivan is quite right in noting that what he calls the "one cause" people are forcing the whole body to address "minority" issues and concerns. But is this necessarily a bad thing?

The apathy of the majority is only one of the factors contributing to the rising chorus of "causes" in our time. A society and a church constructed by "the majority" necessarily create and maintain systems which perpetuate the

---

[1] Timothy J. Sullivan, "The President's Remarks: Public Apathy in American Politics," 1999 Charter Day Commemorative Booklet, College of William and Mary, pp. 11-13.

worldview and interests of that "majority." "Minority" interests must be ignored or suppressed if the *status quo* is to continue.

But minority voices cannot be ignored indefinitely, by society or by the church. We are sent to bring the Good News to everyone. At least since the early 1950s, the Episcopal Church has struggled with what this should mean in a society structured to maintain the world view and interests of a putative "majority."

UNITY AND DIVERSITY

Does the Episcopal Church welcome "the majority"? Who does that include, or not include? In the 1950s and 60s, racial divisions were the focus of this struggle. In the 1970s and 80s, women's "proper place" took center stage. Increasingly in the 1990s, and I'm sure well into the next millenium, sexuality is and will remain the defining issue.

Convention Journals and Executive Council minutes document a half-century of effort—theological, spiritual, institutional, political—to discern God's will for the church more clearly in each of these areas. By no means is this work completed, but at least we continue to struggle with it. From that struggle, perhaps, can come lessons of value to the wider society.

The Scripture is full of stories of God's abundance and the diversity of creation. So long as "the majority" is defined to exclude categories of people, the church cannot realize the fullness of its mission, "to restore all people to unity with God and each other in Christ." As we wrestle with the tensions between unity and diversity let's be aware of our responsibility, not only within the Church, but also as leaven, salt, light to the world around us. ✠

Opening Up the System

CHALLENGE TO POLITICS AS WE KNEW IT
Post-Convention Report, Fall 1991

Was the 70th General Convention a light that failed? Or did it do a creditable job with some very difficult matters? Legislatively, the Convention was cautious—and should have been. It was affected by the transitions which have been taking place in the church, which, among other things, make the legislative process work differently.

We're a more fervent church. People are less tolerant of back-room leadership and private deals. Both Houses of the Convention have changed, because different kinds of people are being elected to the episcopate, and as deputies. The polite but sometimes vicious clubbiness which used to characterize the Bishops is going or gone. Deputies now represent a much broader spectrum of the Church. They may have a better grasp of the mission of the Church, but they have a worse grasp of the legislative process. ☩

CASTING A WIDER NET

Integrity National Convention, San Diego, California, July 17, 1993

I'm sure it seems slow to you, but I do believe we are moving. After my election as President of the House of Deputies, both the Presiding Bishop and I intentionally appointed more Integrity members to Interim Bodies. Their leadership has been superb, and they have made an enormous contribution to the Church. More members of Integrity have been elected as Deputies to the next General Convention, and I shall certainly consider appointing them to legislative committees of the 1994 Convention. But I need your help in this. I need you to tell me about the persons I don't know. ☩

INTENTIONS MISUNDERSTOOD

Statement on Appointment Policy, September 1993

Press accounts of my address to the Integrity Convention in July 1993 have led some to suppose that I intend to "stack" 1994 General Convention legislative committees with Integrity members to the exclusion of those holding other points of view. Nothing could be further from the truth, and I want to set the record straight regarding my appointment practices and intentions.

As President of the House of Deputies, I am responsible for appointing lay and clerical members of the Interim Bodies which study issues and develop policy and program recommendations to bring to General Convention, and also for appointments of Convention deputies to serve on 26

House of Deputies Legislative Committees which consider those recommendations during the Convention itself. By canon, interim body appointments are generally for six years, with half the membership appointed each triennium—about 200 clergy and lay persons, and about 100 bishops (appointed by the Presiding Bishop). House of Deputies Legislative Committee members—more than 500 persons in 1991, serve only during the Convention, and are appointed in January of Convention year.

How Names are Solicited

In fulfilling these appointment responsibilities, I have widely solicited and always welcome suggestions of qualified persons from all quarters of the Church. I have given particular attention to identifying competent people from groups which have previously been under-represented in our leadership and decision-making processes, seeking balance in terms of gender, racial/ethnic identity, geography and ideology. I have received suggestions of persons representing the interests of groups as diverse as Episcopalians United and Integrity, the Episcopal Synod of America and the Episcopal Women's Caucus, NOEL and the Union of Black Episcopalians. Most of my appointments to the 1991-94 Interim Bodies were made in the fall of 1991. I sought persons whose interests and expertise were appropriate to the responsibilities of each interim body, and whose diverse perspectives and willingness to work respectfully with those who oppose their views would enrich the work those groups do on behalf of the rest of the Church.

It was in this context that I assured the Integrity Convention that I do not exclude openly gay and lesbian Episcopalians from consideration for appointments to Interim Bodies or Legislative Committees (as was done in the past). I asked those present to tell me about the qualifications of deputies I might not know, just as I asked members of the

National Network of Episcopal Clergy Associations earlier in the summer, and as I encourage members of others I meet with to make suggestions for appointments.

It grieves me that some have read this invitation to broader participation as a threat to exclude other groups. I reiterate my welcome of suggestions from all constituencies within the Church, and ask your prayers that we may all listen for the voice of the Spirit through the clamor of our public debate. ✠

ONE CHALLENGE OF DIVERSITY
Letter to Deputies and Alternates, September 23, 1993

I want to alert you all to a concern identified at the last Convention, the challenging aspect of what is overall a very positive development.

The steady trend in the House of Deputies toward a more representative and diverse membership, with greater turnover and less longevity among deputies, produces a vibrant, imaginative and energetic legislative body, but one with less depth of procedural expertise and historical perspective. One unfortunate consequence in Phoenix was the consumption of an inordinate amount of precious legislative time dealing with how-to questions from new deputies.

If you have a procedural question during a legislative session, try first to find an answer from experienced members of your own or neighboring deputations, or from specially identified "senior deputies" who will be located around the floor, taking the time of the whole House only as a last resort for questions of major importance. Careful advance preparation, and pooling expertise within your deputation, will contribute to efficient sessions in which time can be devoted to thoughtful debate about substance rather than procedure. ✠

ROLE OF SENIOR DEPUTIES

Invitation to "Senior Deputies", May 26, 1994

We have been working to streamline legislative procedures, improve the committee process, and simplify paperwork through expanded use of computer support. We also hope to improve efficiency on the floor, especially by curbing misuse of "personal privilege" and by discouraging newer deputies from taking the time of the whole House with elementary questions about process. I hope you will serve as part of the second level of a three-tiered strategy to save the microphones for debate. We will ask all deputies to take question about process to:

- first, the chair and other experienced members of their own deputations;

- second, a nearby "Senior Deputy"—you and about forty others who will be introduced on the opening day, your deputations located throughout the floor;

- third, if time allows and the question warrants, the Parliamentarian.

WELCOMING NEWCOMERS BY
SHARING EXPERTISE

If everyone uses these channels for assistance before approaching a microphone, we will save a great deal of legislative time. Most questions can be dealt with at the first level, since few deputations are devoid of parliamentary wisdom.

Some matters are complex and would benefit from wider consultation, and the dynamics of some issues may occasionally make it easier for a deputy to seek advice from outside her/his deputation. I do not expect Senior Deputies to become political strategists advocating the causes of everyone who comes to you for advice, but rather to offer fair-minded procedural or parliamentary guidance as you are able, individually or in consultation with other Senior Deputies.

I hope you will be willing to share your own experience and to pass along the expertise and lore of the House to our newer colleagues. ✠

DEFENDING AN OPEN PROCESS

Correspondence—May 1994

I am sorry you are still concerned about my appointment policies in relation to various groups within the church. Let me try to clarify the situation. Some meetings I attend because they are a part of my official duties—Executive Council, various Standing Commissions, Provincial Synods, the House of Bishops, the Anglican Consultative Council, and so forth. As my schedule permits, I also respond to invitations to preach or speak to other groups, including diocesan conventions, and such unofficial organizations as the National Network of Episcopal Clergy Associations, the Conference of Diocesan Executives, the Urban Caucus, the Consortium of Endowed Parishes, Integrity. I have not been invited to speak to any of the groups listed on your post card.

In the brief period between my election as President and the appointment of Interim Body members for the 1991-94 triennium, I canvassed individuals—deputies, bishops, members of official and unofficial organizations, staff—from a broad spectrum of the church for suggestions, welcoming both their responses and those sent spontaneously from others. There was not time, nor was there any precedent, for officially requesting suggestions from unofficial organizations for that round of Interim Body appointments.

A New Precedent for Openness

There is time for such canvassing of organizations regarding appointments of Deputies to 1994 Legislative Committees, and I chose to implement such a process. Late last spring I began requesting suggestions from every group I met with, and after the majority of dioceses reported their 1994 deputy elections, I wrote to more than two dozen organizations (including all those you list) inviting them to suggest deputies whose interests and expertise are appropriate to particular Legislative Committees, and also asking them to share my request with other interested groups or individuals.

As painful as controversy can be, I believe it is essential to encourage all voices to be heard in our legislative process, and I will do my best to facilitate this through the appointment process. I hope you will join me in praying that God will support us all in serving our beloved Church. ✠

Interim Body Appointments— The Process

Executive Council, Providence, Rhode Island, February 15, 1995

One of the most important duties the Presiding Officers share each triennium is the appointment of persons to serve on the various interim bodies of the General Convention— the standing committees and commissions, boards and other agencies which develop policy and in some instances carry out program, reporting and making recommendations to the next Convention. Including those whose membership is elected, there are 35 such groups. Not many people seem aware of how this process actually works, and I want to describe it briefly for you, in hopes that you will share this information within your own networks.

The canons specify the size and composition—that is, the

proportion of bishops, priests or deacons, and lay people—of each interim body, and occasionally specify some other qualifications. Within those limits, it has long been customary for the appointing officers to attempt to provide some balance geographically, to encourage the involvement of people from every province in the work of the interim bodies. In addition, we make a deliberate effort to identify competent people from groups previously under-represented in our leadership and decision-making processes, seeking balance in terms of gender, racial/ethnic identity, and point of view. Bishop Browning, of course, has a fixed pool of bishops from which to make all his appointments, but there are many thousands of potential clerical and lay appointees. The problem is finding them, and matching them to actual vacancies.

Before Convention I wrote to dozens of organizations inviting them to recommend persons for appointment to specific groups, and recommendation forms were distributed in Indianapolis. Almost 600 forms were returned, in addition to dozens of other suggestions by way of letters and phone calls. Matching up over 700 names with 82 clerical and 107 lay positions to be filled, to provide competent leadership and a diversity of perspectives while achieving some sort of geographical, gender and ethnic balance, was more than a little challenging!

SOME PROGRESS

Despite the difficulties, I am reasonably satisfied with the balance achieved by now, at least in some areas. 30% of the clerical members on interim bodies are women, and of those whose race or ethnicity is known, 22% are not white. Of lay members, 30% are women and 32% minorities. Provincial representation and diocesan distribution are as broad as we could make them.

The most problematic area is that of point of view, in part because it is difficult to achieve diversity without inappropriately labeling or stereotyping people. I had hoped to overcome some of this by inviting recommendations from a broad spectrum of organizations. Unfortunately, only a few responded, at least in an identifiable way, and most were from what might be called the progressive wing of the church. Only a few of the hundreds of people recommended could be identified as representing more conservative views, which severely handicapped my efforts to provide balance on individual interim bodies.

There was one other guideline that we employed in appointments this time, and that was to broaden our leadership and cultivate a new generation by trying not to put people on more than one body and minimizing reappointments to ensure a steady flow of fresh ideas and energy while maintaining essential continuity. This was one of the most personally difficult and risk-filled aspects of the whole process.

Making appointments is always fraught with peril, and results are guaranteed to produce some slighted feelings. With a fixed number of positions, it is inevitable that the inclusion of new groups reduces the number of those from groups which have traditionally dominated our institutional life. I hope you will help me to share information about the rationale and process for appointments, and let me know any ideas you have about improving the way it is done. ✠

Will you persevere in resisting evil,
and when you fall into sin,
repent and return to the Lord?
—Book of Common Prayer, p. 304

Persevere in Resisting Evil

CHOOSE LOVE, NOT HATE
1993 Integrity National Convention, San Diego, California,
July 17, 1993

If we can love ourselves, then we can begin to love one another. It has been said that we are living in a time of violence, and even the network producers have finally admitted that violence on the television screen is having a harmful effect. I recently heard it said that love is not an emotion but a disciplined act of will. We choose to love, and, as John tells us in his letter, "love must not be a matter of words or talk. Love must be genuine and show itself in action" (I John 3:18-19). There are many forms of violence; only one is physical. Hatred is a form of violence. When one hates, one is engaging in violence. If we are sowing love where there is hatred, we are turning upside down the violence that is in our church and our society because violence is ultimately a form of hatred. ✠

POTENTIAL FOR EVIL LURKS

Statement on the death of Matthew Shepard, October 12, 1998

Matthew Shepard was pistol whipped, burned and left for dead, tied like a crucified scarecrow to a rancher's fence on the outskirts of Laramie, Wyoming. The apparent motive for his savage murder was hatred because Shepard was gay.

Four months earlier, James Byrd, Jr., was beaten and tied by his ankles to the back of pick-up truck, dragged two or three miles down a road in Jasper County, east Texas till there was nothing left to recognize as human. The apparent motive for his savage murder was hatred because Byrd was black.

These horrifying crimes, committed under cover of darkness on lonely country roads, warn of the potential for evil that lurks in every town and city, and in our churches, too. We must take the message of these hate crimes seriously—our faith requires it, and our survival as a civilization depends on it.

As members of Matthew Shepard's church, Episcopalians must proclaim again the conviction first expressed by our General Convention in 1976, that "homosexual persons are children of God who have a full and equal claim with all other persons upon the love, acceptance, and pastoral concern and care of the Church," and "are entitled to equal protection of the laws with all other citizens."

Matthew is now far beyond the inadequate shelter of protective laws. His nightmare is over, and he is safe in the arms of his Creator. We who remain must redouble our efforts to proclaim that the Matthew Shepard's and the James Byrd's of this world are all fully and equally children of God. We must redouble our efforts to ensure equal protection under the law for every person in this nation.

Most of all, we must redouble our efforts to bring the healing love of Christ into a fearful and hate-ridden world. May God have mercy on us all. ✠

THE STRUGGLE TO CHANGE HEARTS

Executive Council, Oklahoma City, Oklahoma, November 3, 1998

Early in the summer I participated in two events dealing with an issue dear to my heart—an old issue, from some perspectives, but with fresh meaning today. In June, along with Dean Martha Horne and Bishop Mary Adelia McLeod, I was "Exhibit A" at a conference on Southern Episcopal Women's History. In July I was honored to preach at the dedication of an icon of Elizabeth Cady Stanton, as part of the 150th Anniversary of the first Women's Rights Convention in Seneca Falls, New York.

Both meetings, in different ways, provided opportunity to look back at where we have been and to celebrate the opening of many areas of social, political and religious life to women. Both also were full of reminders about the many ways in which women still suffer from centuries of second class status. As with racism, so with sexism: eliminating the legal barriers to discrimination does not by itself change hearts. And as we know, in the church even the legal barriers against ordained women, or women seeking ordination, have not yet been wholly removed.

Participating in those meetings about women gave a special framework to the event that was just hitting the papers: the murder of James Byrd, a black man tied to the back of a truck and dragged to death. It happened in Jasper County in east Texas, a place which had prided itself on good race relations, with a black mayor and white sheriff. But good laws and enlightened leadership are not enough to overcome the evil that often lurks in human hearts.

They are not enough when it comes to race, or to sex, or to sexual orientation, especially when deeply-held religious convictions are added to the mix. And then we heard the appalling news of a gay young Episcopalian beaten and left to die in Wyoming. These things all came together for me, and I met with the International and National Concerns

Committee of Executive Council to talk about how we might develop a concerted response. Here is part of what I said to them:

A CONCERN HEAVY ON MY HEART

The lingering cancer of racism prompts our on-going anti-racism program. Though our efforts are still far from enough, I am proud of the Episcopal Church's long record in grappling with the issue of racism and its effects on the lives of us all. We've been brave and persistent, and I trust will continue to be so. But racism and sexism are only a part of the picture.

I cannot tell you how appalled I was by the savage murder of Matthew Shepard, a young Episcopal college student who was pistol whipped and hung on a fence to die. Everyone was, of course. It's sickening to realize that anyone could do such a thing to another human being. But I am also struck by the degree to which this young man's death has touched a chord and served as a catalyst—not just for memorial services and candlelight vigils around the country, but for serious political organizing in support of broadly-inclusive bias crime legislation throughout the country.

HOW SHOULD WE RESIST HATE

It's ironic that just a few days before Matthew was attacked, the Diocese of Wyoming had petitioned the state legislature to pass a hate crimes measure. Many states don't yet have such legislation, and less than half of those which do include sexual orientation as a protected class. I know that some dispute the appropriateness of anti-hate legislation. Obviously legislation does not change what's in people's hearts, and it's doubtful a Wyoming statute would have protected Matthew Shepard from his assailants. Neverthe-less, there is something here that we dare not ignore.

Across the street from St. Mark's Episcopal Church in Caspar, Wyoming, a small group of protestors from Kansas carried signs and shouted slogans while Matthew's funeral was going on. "God hates fags." "Matthew is in hell"—the sort of things that same group says when they picket us at General Convention. They are so extreme that most people quickly dismiss them. But not everyone. Fred Phelps' followers are only the most visible of the hate-mongers, and by no means the only ones to misuse the Holy Scriptures and the name of God to advance their evil cause. Last week's murder of Dr. Barnett Slepian in Buffalo, NY, appears to be another vile example of people driven to murderous action by absolutist interpretations of Scripture and a moral code which has no room for disagreement.

AN EPISCOPAL WITNESS

I would like to see the Episcopal Church become more visible in the effort to reclaim the authority of Scripture from its misuse by the extreme right-wing. The spontaneous vigils and demonstrations surrounding Matthew Shepard's death suggest that many other Episcopalians feel the same way. Bishop Griswold and I both issued statements following Matthew's death, but we need actions to back up our words.

So I am suggesting today that we give serious attention to what we can do as a Church—carefully, not in blind reaction to something dreadful, but thoughtfully, responsibly, in a manner respectful of the fact that not all Episcopalians agree about homosexuality, though all deplore Matthew's murder. Let us do it in the spirit of that portion of the Lambeth sexuality resolution which acknowledges that we are all children of God, and invites us to serious dialogue. Let us do it in a way which encourages seeing the connections between all forms of discrimination and oppression. ☩

COMMISSIONING FOR A JUBILEE YEAR

Jubilee 2000 Conference, Kanuga Conference Center,
Hendersonville, North Carolina, December 4, 1999

We have come here to celebrate Jubilee 2000, to immerse ourselves in the meaning of Jubilee and to commit ourselves to working for a Jubilee Year. We have come here from around the country, from the midst of our own busy lives, to find energy, ideas, resources, but above all to find community: colleagues to share in the work, soul-mates to inspire and comfort, to keep us going through discouragement, to share joys and disappointments, to remind us of why we are doing this hard work in the first place.

We must be community for each other, because "back home," wherever that may be, our work is likely to bring us into conflict with the comfortable and the powerful, with the complacent and the wealthy, with principalities and powers. Look at the people on either side of you. I mean, really look at them. They are community and support for you, and you must be community and support for them. Are you ready to commit to that?

Among us are individuals and groups committed to many different activities which hasten "the year of the Lord's favor"—the work of anti-racism, and against discrimination of any kind, influencing public policy, addressing the many forms of economic injustice, working for peace at home and around the world, "greening the Church" to save the earth from ourselves—all vital, noble, difficult work in the footsteps of Jesus who made Isaiah's claim his own.

THE COST OF FOLLOWING JESUS

When Jesus read that passage announcing the beginning of his life's work, people were at first amazed, and then indignant, and then violently hostile. We must expect the same if we choose to follow his example.

When we look around and see all the wrongs in this world, wrongs we know God calls us to set right, we need to remember how they got that way, lest we charge off on our white horses, ill-prepared, and end up burned out and bewildered when things don't get "fixed" right away.

Most of the conditions we seek to change developed because they benefited somebody. So, like Jesus in Nazareth, we must expect the same resistance he encountered: amazement that we dare to challenge the status quo, indignation at the disruption we're likely to cause, and finally, violent hostility, to defend the present order with all its privileges.

Several years ago, I was privileged to address the national convention of Integrity, meeting in San Diego. I spoke about several aspects of the church vis a vis sexuality and "traditional" norms. I promised to consider recommendations from Integrity for appointments to committees of Convention, as I promise every group I meet. I also shared a personal story about my own son, whose stellar career had just been brutally interrupted when he was denied partnership in his law firm solely because he was gay.

AMAZEMENT, INDIGNATION AND HOSTILITY

I am happy to be able to report today that he has since become partner in another prestigious firm. That, of course, is not really the point. The point is that his gifts were ultimately recognized for what they truly are, and another small step was taken on the road to justice. But I will never forget my own sense of rage and helplessness over my son's experience of stupid injustice, and I bring it up again today because the aftermath of that address illustrates so well the patterns of amazement, indignation and hostility that mark resistance to change.

A conservative publication headlined an article about that meeting, and my speech, "Ethics by Anecdote." A bishop, whom I had considered a friend, wrote an outraged letter to the Living Church excoriating what he had heard—not read—about my address, and suggesting that my performance as President of the House of Deputies would be biased against traditional morality. He didn't even call to ask for a copy, to see what I, his "friend," had actually said, before blasting me in print. A priest wrote a long letter dripping with anger and contempt, concluding with the suggestion that I seek counseling from my rector who would be able to help my "dysfunctional family."

Knowing my pain as the earthly mother to my son, think of God's pain when any child of God is treated in a less than Christian way. Amazement, indignation, hostility are the price we must always expect to pay when we seek to right wrongs and address injustice.

You know all this. You have experienced it. Some may even be on the edge of burn-out. We come here to refocus our commitment, and to recharge our batteries so we can return to the struggle. As we prepare for that return, I'd like to broaden our awareness of what we struggle against. Principalities and powers, yes. People and institutions vested in the present order, yes. Ignorance, desperation, hatred, yes. But there is more.

The Lord has sent me to bring good news to the oppressed, to bind up the broken-hearted, to proclaim liberty to the captives, and release to the prisoners. Generally we hear these words as the job description God hands to us. We use its imperatives to fuel the urgency of our work for justice. We use its images of liberated captives and released prisoners to gather support for the Jubilee 2000 campaign to forgive the staggering debts of "developing" countries. This is a good thing. Lapel pins made of a piece of broken chain are excellent conversation-starters. We are called to help break the chains binding the poor and oppressed in every land.

BREAKING EVERY CHAIN

However, we can only do it if we are also committed to breaking the chains that bind us, individually and institutionally. The oppressed, the broken-hearted, the captives, the prisoners, are not just the objects of our labors. They are ourselves, whom Jesus came to serve.

You are oppressed; what good news will Jesus bring you? You are broken-hearted; how will Jesus bind up your wounds? You are captive; how will Jesus proclaim liberty to you? You are a prisoner; how will Jesus bring your release? What chains bind you, limiting your vision, your energy, your ability to pour yourself into the vital work to which Jesus calls you? What holds you captive—fear of failure? the wrong sort of pride over success? the trappings of privilege? a need for approval? contempt for those who disagree? a Messiah complex?

"Walk humbly with your God," said Micah. It doesn't take much self-scrutiny to bring us to humility before God and a humble attitude of service in our human relationships. To begin to see ourselves as God sees us is to begin to break the chains that bind us.

What of the chains which bind the Church? From the book of Acts to this day, the Church has been vulnerable to the oppression of its own institutional structures, vital as they are to passing the Gospel message from one generation to the next. We must strive for flexibility and the willingness to let things go lest the pillars that have supported us become bars in a prison cell.

MOURNING OUR LOSSES

Is the Church "broken-hearted"? We mourn the loss of stability and certainty, or what we imagine to have been stability and certainty, when we look back nostalgically to the time before we had to assume responsibility for the

Church's life, when bishops were "giants," all holy men, and clergy were all powerful preachers, and lay people were all devout tithers, and Conventions never had to deal with difficult issues.

We grieve the loss of our elders, of those who have "gone before" without leaving us a detailed set of instructions for managing this immense enterprise. Nevertheless, we must not be afraid to shoulder responsibility in our time as they did in theirs. They had no clearer idea of how to lead than we have, and it's our turn now.

Years ago, in the midst of the struggle for the ordination of women, I was talking with Verna Dozier, one of my mentors whose wisdom and fearlessness in addressing injustice are well known to many of you. Full of uncertainty about how best to proceed, assailed by doubts about whether our cause was just, I asked Verna what she thought Jesus would advise about our situation. With a beatific smile, she looked at me and said, "He'd tell a parable, so you'd still have to figure it out for yourself!"

How right she was! We are the elders, and we have to figure things out ourselves. And yet—God has given us the Holy Scriptures and the Church, conveyors of the Good News of our faith. God has given us the example of Jesus's life, and the redeeming power of his death and resurrection. God has given us the constant presence and inspiration of the Holy Spirit, and the astonishing promise that there will be a "year of the Lord's favor," not by our doing, but by the mercy and grace of God.

What a promise! The chains holding us back from that "year of favor" will fall to our feet, ours and those we are commanded to serve. Justice will flow down like a river, and the whole Creation will rejoice as All is reconciled to God.

What a promise! Are you ready? ☩

From the Ozarks to the House of Deputies

Women's Liberation

Christmas Letter, 1973

If this year has had any overall theme, it could be called the Year of Women's Liberation—not that it happened, you understand, but it was what we worked at most. Pam is still President of the Episcopal Churchwomen of the Diocese of Washington, and early in the new year she had to defend the ECW resolution on the ordination of women to the priesthood at the Diocesan Convention. Good old "wishy-washy" Mom (as the children call her) has made so many enemies in the process she has printed a response to letters of complaint which says, "Dear Sir or Madam: Thank you for your crank letter." ✠

A Traditional ECW Background

ECW Communiqué, Winter 1990

"What's a nice girl like you doing in a place like this?" is hardly the greeting I get as I go around the Church these days. By no stretch of the imagination do I still qualify as a "girl."

But I am amazed how many times I am asked, especially by younger women, "How did you get where you are?" In this context, I assume "where you are" means Vice President of the House of Deputies, senior warden, a member of the standing committee of the Anglican Consultative Council, or as Sally Brown often says in Peanuts, "whatever." Behind the question, it oftentimes feels to me, is the implication that like Aphrodite I rose from the sea to be "whatever." Nothing could be further from the truth.

A traditional ECW background can be an invaluable training ground for participation in decision-making bodies at all levels of the church—parish, diocese and national. A little over 25 years ago I attended my first ECW meeting in the Diocese of Washington, as my parish's UTO custodian. In the years since I have discovered many things about the ministries of women. For the most part, the flowered hats have gone, but the dedication and the commitment to mission remain as strong as ever. And I say, "Right on, Sisters!"

As long as men still dominate the Church or politics or any other field—and make no mistake about it, they do—like it or not women will largely have to depend on men to help them enter the system. If [House of Deputies President] Charles Lawrence had not given women an opportunity to perform at the 1985 General Convention, it simply would not have happened. Once given the opportunity, women still have to prove themselves, and because they did not grow up in the system they are handicapped by inexperience. When you're the first, there is added pressure to outperform everybody else simply because you are the first. ✠

SHARING THE JOURNEY

St. Philips Church, Laurel, Maryland, Fall 1991

Our vision of the future is informed and molded by our spiritual journeys. There is a need to share our stories, but I really struggled with that. Part of the struggle was occasioned by the fact that many of us are brought up to believe that it is not "polite" to discuss ourselves and our more intimate thoughts and feelings in public. Difficult as the struggle has proved, it has been a useful process because it has forced me to wrestle with my own experiences in the church, to attempt to articulate my own theology. ✠

A PAINFUL STORY

1993 Integrity National Convention, San Diego, California, July 17, 1993

Not long ago, a wonderful young man I have known since childhood came to me in deep distress. He comes from a good family, received a superior education in church schools and Ivy League colleges, attending one as an undergraduate and graduating from the law school of the second. He graduated Phi Beta Kappa, and has had a brilliant career path. Member of a prestigious law firm, he was on the track to partner. His integrity—and I used that word advisedly—is without question. He is kind, good, the soul of honor, has never been involved in any untoward event. He is gay.

Although he was a regular member of a church growing up, he has stopped attending church now. He was recently told by the review committee of his law firm that they were having second thoughts about making him partner because the question was being asked, "Can we trust him around the clients?" Translate: "Will he try to put the make on a male CEO?"—although there has never been one instance where he did not behave with the utmost propriety.

Before going to that law firm, he clerked for a Supreme Court Justice who was considered to be the swing vote in the Court's consideration of Bowers vs. Hardwick, the George case challenging the sodomy laws in that state. Justices normally assign research on pending cases to any one of their several law clerks. In this case, research was not assigned to this young man, and he had no influence on the Justice's decision in the case.

However, the gay community in Washington held the young man personally responsible for the Justice's decision not to overturn the George statute, and the young man has been told that he is a "pariah" in the gay community. This young man has no home either in the straight community or the gay community. Seeds of love, I am reminded from the Gospel lesson last Sunday, can fall on extremely rocky soil. I know because that young man is my son, and I grieve for his exclusion by both straights and gays. I have not before said publicly anything about my son's sexual orientation, but I do so to you tonight with his permission. ✠

ED BROWNING: PARTNER IN MISSION

Diocese of Chicago Convocation, March 16, 1996

Among the many blessings that have come my way as your President, I count none more valuable than the wonderful personal and professional relationship Bishop Browning and I have established. It is for me an example of the great Anglican principle of "mutual responsibility and interdependence," an on-going experience of collaboration and shared ministry. I give thanks daily for the trust and genuine affection that have grown between us over the years, and our absolute conviction that each is committed to seeking the very best for this Church.

This is a great personal blessing for me, in what is often a lonely job. I also think the way Bishop Browning and I work together offers something very important to the whole church as well. Our joint appearances through the years—in diocesan visitations, at the head table for Executive Council, before the cameras on convention videos and national teleconferences, meeting with committees and commissions, representing our church in the National Council of Churches and the Anglican Consultative Council—all these tasks we have shared say much about this church's commitment to "mutual ministry," to the complementary roles of women and men, laity and clergy, politician and pastor, in our common life.

Neither in our public work together, nor in our many private discussions, do we always agree about the importance of issues or the best strategies for handling them. But we have walked together through the wretched series of crisis and scandal, crime and conflict, that has beset our beloved church, and rejoiced together in such experiences as seeing good ministry done in unlikely places and being proud that our church is not afraid to deal honestly with very important if scary topics.

SHARED COMMITMENT TO WELCOME ALL

We have upheld each other in prayer, frankly shared our thoughts and fears, and supported each other's commitment to keep this church a place of welcome for all. No matter how frustrated or discouraged we sometimes get, no matter how hurt or angry we may feel about the relentless criticism, we can remind each other that GOD has invited absolutely everybody to the great banquet—Bishop Browning, me, you, all the bishops, all the clergy, all the people of this church and every church and no church.

That's where my hope and excitement lie for the Episcopal Church in these closing days of the second millennium, and the thing I like best about being President of the House of Deputies: the people are our greatest sign of hope. As we grow in grace, we come more and more to see that we *do* stand on common ground—the common foundation that is our salvation through CHRIST JESUS. From that unity arises our ability to work side by side to feed the hungry and clothe the naked, to comfort the sick and visit those in prison, to proclaim the good news of JESUS despite all our disagreements.

We are members of one community of faith, accountable to and challenged by each other. When I get weary, or smug and intolerant, and start to thank GOD that I am not like that tax collector over there, you must remind me to say, "GOD be merciful to me a sinner;" and I will endeavor to do that for you. So, together, we answer GOD's call to be faithful in our time as countless generations have been before us. ✠

PEOPLE ARE THE BEST PART

September 1996 Column in Episcopal Life

I am often asked, "What do you like most about being President of the House of Deputies?" I can honestly say it is the people I meet as I travel across the country. They have truly enriched my life, and made me deeply aware of what a privilege it is to be part of this branch of God's Kingdom.

I have been moved and impressed by the level of commitment so many people have to the Episcopal Church. Their dedication to the Church, as Christ's body here on earth, expresses profound love for our Lord and acceptance of our baptismal duty to spread the Good News of the Gospel.

That is, after all, the only good reason for enduring the major crises and the minor frustrations of our life together— in our congregations and dioceses, and in the national life of the Church. God calls us into loving relationship with each other, so that God's own love for all can be made known. ✠

EXECUTIVE COUNCIL AS COMMUNITY

Executive Council, Toronto, Ontario, November 9,1996
Joint Meeting with Anglican Church of Canada

It is good to be with you again after missing the June meeting in Charleston. In the 17 years I've been attending Executive Council meetings—six years as an elected member, six years as Vice President and five years so far as President of the House of Deputies—I've only missed two meetings. One was for the death of a close family member and the other when I was in Capetown, South Africa, for an Anglican Consultative Council meeting.

This community has become very important to me. By now I must have spent several months of my life in your company! I missed you in June, and was deeply touched that so many of you called or sent cards, letters and even e-mail messages. ✠

SHARING LEADERSHIP

Executive Council, Honolulu, April 26, 1997

The final meeting of any triennium is bittersweet: but this time there is a very special poignancy, because it is the last time we shall meet under the leadership of Edmond L. Browning, our beloved Presiding Bishop these last twelve years. Ed Browning, with the steadfast support of Patti and her own remarkable ministry at home and abroad, has presided over a remarkable period in the life of our church.

Not often in any lifetime do we have the opportunity to be led by a person of great humility, the utmost integrity, and a very real vision of what God is calling us—as a Church, and as individuals—to be. Not often are we privileged to share so closely in the hard decisions, the revelations and insights, the moments of grace as we seek God's will through the thicket of difficult problems and pressures from every side.

When I was elected vice-president of the House of Deputies, Ed, as the new Presiding Bishop, asked me to chair a special Committee for the Full Participation of Women in the Church. He also invited me to take a seat on the Executive Council. From that vantage point I was able to witness his dedication to listening to the many voices of our Church, and his faith that within the sometimes noisy hubbub it was possible to discern the voice of God.

Some of you remember that I had served a term on Council just prior to Ed's election. His invitation that, as vice-president, I continue with a seat and voice in this body enabled me to see clearly how he put his own stamp on Council's life and work, and to learn from his quiet convictions and courageous commitments.

Then during six years as President of the House of Deputies I have been deeply blessed to be included in a real partnership, as we struggled to provide the best leadership to this Church. Not everyone has liked every decision; but I can assure you that every one of them was made with careful consultation, fervent prayer, and a sincere devotion to the well-being of this Church as an agent of the Gospel in our world. ✠

FAREWELL TRIBUTE TO
EDMOND L. BROWNING

72nd General Convention, Philadelphia, Pennsylvania, July 20, 1997

I have seen Bishop Browning struggle with crisis after crisis, never losing his courage, and never failing to keep the course he had set for himself and for this Church.

We have been blessed as a Church by his courage and devotion, and by his deep spirituality; by his steadfast attention to things that were not only difficult for the Church but personally very painful to him; and I rejoice that I have been privileged to share in his prophetic leadership.

Thank you, Ed, for all that you have shared with me, and thank you for your inspiring example of faithfulness in the midst of great adversity. I trust your legacy will continue into the next chapter in our church's life.

Let us honor Ed Browning by making his values of empathic listening and prayerful discernment an on-going aspect of this Church's way of doing business.

Let us honor Ed Browning by holding fast to his conviction that God calls and loves absolutely everybody, and speaks to us especially through the voices of the poor and the outcast.

Let us honor Ed Browning by continuing his commitment to re-form the church so that all are welcomed, nurtured, challenged by the baptismal covenant, and sent forth to spread the Good News from a loving home base within the community of faith.

In the long long life of the Church, what we do here at the close of the second millenium is only a blip on the timeline. But we are the people of a God who numbers the sparrows and counts the hairs on our heads.

Working with Ed has given me a deepening appreciation of God's boundless love and compassion, and a commitment to continuing his witness to inclusivity, and the full participation of all in the life of the Church.

I am personally thankful for the many blessings that have come to me through this partnership with the Presiding Bishop. I also hope and believe that we have set an example of shared ministry—lay and ordained, male and female—that will inspire others not only within the Episcopal Church but also throughout the Anglican Communion and among fellow Christians everywhere. ✠

My Life In the Church

Celebration of Southern Episcopal Church Women
Kanuga Conference Center,
Hendersonville, North Carolina, June 6, 1998

Once upon a time in the Ozark Mountains of Southwest Missouri, four Short men married four Long women. I am not referring to the height of the actors, but rather to their last names! Four sisters named Long married three brothers and a cousin named Short.

From one of those couples issued my mother, and I suppose I could say, "that's the long and the short of it," and sit down! But instead, I'll try to answer this question: How did a mountain girl get from a small Ozark town to the podium of the House of Deputies of the Episcopal Church, presiding over an assembly twice the size of the town in which she was reared?

It was a long journey, and oftentimes a painful journey—not so much in the miles covered (though in recent years I've accumulated more frequent flyer miles than I care to think about), but rather in the immense social, emotional and spiritual distances that separate my life today from that of my very-small-town southern childhood.

A Checkered Career

First, let me say that I have had a rather checkered career, in life and in the church. I graduated from college with a B.S. degree in psychology, expecting to teach a year or two, marry, settle down in the suburbs, raise a family, and be a perfect mother.

Feminism came to me rather late in life, but it did come to me through the church, both directly and tangentially. It was a long process of growth and pain, and a spiritual journey I would divide into three phases: (1) discovery of self; (2) discovery of women and men in community;

(3) finally, partly as a result of marvelous experiences such as going to South Africa in 1983 to testify for Bishop Desmond Tutu, the discovery of going beyond community to be the Body of Christ in the world.

EARLY YEARS—DISCOVERY OF SELF

Some years ago I came across a quote in a novel—I no longer remember which novel—that has stayed with me because it spoke so directly to my situation. In it the narrator says, "My mother was of that lost generation of women, born in the twenties, too young to be flappers or suffragettes, and too old to be liberated superwomen of the sixties-turned-seventies." I belong somewhere in that lost generation.

I was born and brought up in Springfield, a very small town in the Ozark mountains of southwest Missouri. Ours was a strict but loving extended family household, but I observed very early on that there was definitely a double standard for males and females. While men ruled the roost, it was the women who were the strong ones behind the scenes. It was the women who modeled the values, imposed the discipline, went to church, fed the hoboes who came to the kitchen door, looked after the sick, and kept the family together.

My family believed firmly in education—even for girls!—and felt that children should go to college in another part of the country to broaden their perspective. They also felt that a coeducational college was a better choice than an all-girls school, so my cousin Ann and I were sent off to the College of William and Mary in Virginia.

At least we were in another part of the country; but we might as well have been in a girls' school, because all the men went off to World War II during our freshman year, and didn't return until the last semester of our senior year. In spite of the War, however, and the restrictions inherent in the prevailing doctrine of in loco parentis, we managed to have a reasonably good time, and to obtain a good education—which we were not expected to use for any purpose other than our own amusement.

EDUCATED...FOR WHAT?

After college, we made a few half-hearted attempts at a career, but women really weren't expected nor encouraged to do much else but get married and raise a family. My own mother had had to go to work when my father disappeared from our lives, and this probably added to the ambivalence, teaching me unconsciously that women only worked outside the home if catastrophe had struck.

On the other hand, she was very bright, strong and competent, and after I went off to William and Mary she moved east also, to Washington DC where my uncle had become a member of the United States House of Representatives. Mother worked in his office, his de facto chief of staff for many years, and during the summers cousin Ann and I had jobs in congressional offices too. Through these connections, after graduation I got a "real job" doing psychological research for the Air Force, and then returned to William and Mary for a year as an instructor in psychology.

There was never any doubt, however, that as soon as marriage became an option the job would be history! And so it was. I did just what I was "supposed" to do: I married, moved to the suburbs, raised a family and was the perfect mother! Well, at least I produced two perfect children, whose accomplishments continue to swell my mother-heart with pride, amazement and gratitude.

Part of doing the suburban family thing in the fifties and sixties was being active at church. I had discovered the Episcopal Church at William and Mary, and was confirmed by Bishop Francis Craighill at Bruton Parish during my freshman year there. As a young suburban matron I was happy to throw myself into church activities, not just because it was something to do but because the Church was already very important to me.

WOMEN AND MEN IN COMMUNITY

Historically, most women's activity in the church was channeled through some kind of separate women's organizations, since women were excluded from formal leadership roles. Only recently can we see how those segregated organizational structures were preparing women to move into positions of leadership and influence within the whole Church.

When I first began to feel a vocation to "do something" about, for, and in the Church, the options for service were many—but they were mostly in the kitchen. Don't get me wrong—I am not knocking the kitchen. I met most of my best friends there. But there were not many—if any—decision-making jobs open to women in the Church.

When my husband and I first became active in our parish, he was asked to be on the vestry, and I was asked to be UTO custodian. I still have a very special feeling about the United Thank Offering and the enormous good it does. But once I became involved, I was struck by the curious paradox that the institution of the Church, which is ordinarily alert to racial prejudice and other social injustices, was so completely unaware of the prejudices operating against women. Indeed, where the Church should have been leading the way, we often find it lagging far behind the rest of society.

Most all of us, in those days, did what we could within the existing structures, and gradually began to articulate our dissatisfaction and sense that God was calling the Church to something better. When our diocesan canons were changed to permit women to be elected to the Vestry, I was elected. And I stuck with it. Women have tenacity, which leads me to the observation that one reason women have a reasonable degree of success despite the odds is because they have been willing to hang in instead of dropping out. Men came and went on the vestry, but I wouldn't go away, and when my parish didn't know what else to do with me, they elected me senior warden—the first woman to hold that position in the Diocese of Washington.

"DEAR BROTHER"

I occupied that position for the five years allowed by the by-laws, but was kept humble by the Bishop's annual letter to Wardens bearing the salutation: "Dear Brother." The first year, I circled it, returned it to him and noted that there were now wardens who were not "brothers." The next year, the same thing happened. Again I responded and finally, after three years, the salutation was changed to read, "Dear Warden.". A small victory, perhaps, this change of a single word—but it spoke volumes about our changing awareness— my own, and that of the church around me.

When I became president of the diocesan ECW in 1972, we had begun the fight for the ordination of women. Our diocese and our ECW were plunged right into the middle of the battle. It was not an easy time for us as an organization, or for me personally. The ECW had never before taken controversial stands. We were expected to raise the money and make the tea, but leave the business of running the church to "the boys." The rest of the diocese was startled to see us behaving so differently, and not everyone in the ECW was comfortable with this new role.

For me personally it was a very painful time. I had been raised to believe that women didn't make waves, and one certainly didn't take issue with the male authority structure. During this time I met a young priest who, after working with me on a project, expressed surprise that we had had such an agreeable relationship. He said he had been told in seminary to avoid the President of the ECW like the plague! Things like that hurt. But with the pain came growth, and each confrontation became a little easier, and less painful. I finally came to the realization that no matter how hard I tried, not everyone in the world was going to like me, and it was more important that I like myself.

A LAYWOMAN'S STAKE IN THE ORDINATION OF WOMEN

As I became convinced of the rightness of the ordination of women and committed to working for it, a whole new world opened to me. I had found a cause for which I was ready to risk and fight. Tied up inextricably in that campaign was the issue of the rights of all women—lay and ordained—in the Church. Many people hear the phrase "women's rights" as something selfish and unchristian, putting the individual before the community. Like many other women, I had to struggle against this negative judgment. It was not an easy time for me, having been brought up on "white gloves and party manners," with a deeply-instilled awe of the male authority figure and the belief that the only proper role for a woman was that of wife and mother. But through the struggle I came to see that "rights" have to do with what is right—with what is in accord with the justice God wills for all relationships in the Body of Christ, and in the world.

Still, it was difficult learning to make waves, and I can remember sitting at my typewriter in the summer of 1976, writing a speech on sexism in the church which I was to give at the Minneapolis General Convention, while my son, who was entering college in the fall, was sewing name tapes on his clothes. I felt so guilty that I wasn't sewing them on for him; but the fact that he was and I wasn't was tremendous progress for both of us!

CHURCH SEXIST, CHINNIS SAYS

The 1976 Triennial Meeting of the Women of the Church, for which I was Presiding Officer, had as its theme, "Standing in the Midst." We were truly standing in the midst of enormous changes, not only in the life of our Church but also in the lives of women generally. After years of trial texts, that Convention was to vote on a new Book of Common Prayer, and we also faced another critical vote on the ordination of women.

Although I was perceived by some diocesan ECW presidents as a flaming liberal, all was going well until the day I was asked to be on a panel on sexism sponsored by *The Witness.* The headline on the front page of the Convention Daily the next day was, "Church Sexist, Chinnis Says." The Triennial planning consultant wished she could get a muzzle for me!

As we stood in the midst of Triennial 1976, I experienced the transformation that can take place as we try to live out our lives with others called to be on the same path with whom I might not agree. It meant learning to live by love, and learning to be persons in community with other persons for the sake of the larger mission of reconciliation. It demanded a commitment to personal growth, and learning to sacrifice and love more fully.

This process of transformation is not without pain. In becoming open to all that is new, there is pain in letting go of that which is old. Sometimes the things that hurt us the most are the hardest to discard. The promise is that in the struggle—the constant, changing struggle for growth—God is always present.

VIM AND PORT ST. LUCIE

Because of my involvement with the Triennial Meeting in 1976, I was asked by then Presiding Bishop John Allin to be vice chairperson of the Cabinet of Venture in Mission. Naturally, a bishop (one I liked very much), was the Chairman. When he resigned because of pressures and reasons of health, I, as vice-chairman, was not asked to move up, but a layman was brought in as chair. But tenacity and persistence paid off: his term was short-lived and the woman vice chair became, in his words, "the third titular head" of the Cabinet of Venture in Mission!

Before this had happened there was an even more significant crisis, for me, regarding this assignment. In 1977, the Venture in Mission Cabinet was meeting in conjunction with the House of Bishops in Port St. Lucie, Florida. You may remember that it was during this meeting that Bishop Allin announced he could not accept the ordination of women, which had been approved by the previous General Convention, and asked whether the House of Bishops wanted him to resign. Instead of accepting his resignation, the bishops adopted a "statement of conscience" which in effect gave each other permission to ignore the Church's lawfully-enacted canons.

I was appalled by this development, and stayed up half the night agonizing over whether I should resign my Venture in Mission position as protest. The next morning, at breakfast with the VIM chair, my friend Bishop Keller, and his wife, I shared my anguish and intention to resign. They understood fully, but in the end helped me decide to continue. I will never forget sitting there in the early morning sunshine as Polly Keller helped me see the importance of staying the course—using the position I had managed to achieve to work for change from within, while others continued the struggle from outside the institutional structures. It was one of the hardest decisions I have ever made.

Why did I keep hanging on? I submit to you—even two decades later—that it will still be a long time before women are elected in great numbers to decision-making positions in the Church. Until such time, we must take advantage of whatever avenues we can to achieve positions of influence, to work twice as hard in them, and prove to men, to other women, and to ourselves, that we can do just as good a job—if not better!

It was not until 1970 that women could be seated In the House of Deputies of the General Convention. Twenty-one years later, in 1991, I became the first woman to be elected President of that august body, and I am enormously proud of that honor and what it represents about the expanding role of women in our Church. Nevertheless, it is still harder for women, especially clergywomen, to be elected, and the House of Deputies still bears many characteristics of an exclusive men's club. This is even more true of the House of Bishops, to which 8 women have been elected in the past ten years compared with more than 100 men.

INNER BARRIERS TO CHANGE

It may well be that the most blatant forms of bias are behind us, but I think they may have been the easier ones to fight. Now, the most significant obstacles are the inner barriers—inner barriers for men and women both, that have been bred into us by generations of acculturation. These are more subtle, harder to identify, not as easy to confront, and far more difficult to root out.

When I was invited to join the Chapter of the National Cathedral in Washington, I inquired about the contributions I might be able to make, and was told that the Chapter needed to be reminded constantly that there were women in the world who could make a real contribution in decision-making bodies. "Okay," I said, "I can buy that." Then, at the first meeting I attended, this very same person said, "Members of the Chapter and their wives are invited on a special tour of the Cathedral." Not so innocently, I asked if those of us who had no wives could bring our husbands.

Like the "Dear Brother" letter to Wardens, this was evidence of the way people still unconsciously presume that those in power are men, and women are all "merely wives." I had a similar experience just this spring, when Bishop Griswold and I represented the Episcopal Church at the launching of the new Anglican Province of Central America. Phoebe Griswold had asked for time with the wives of the Central American bishops, to talk about their roles in preparation for a paper she is doing for the Spouses Conference at Lambeth this summer. I was looking forward to a tour of various mission works in San Jose scheduled for the rest of us that morning. Can you guess what happened? I was put into a car with "the women" and had to spend three hours listening to conversation about being a bishop's wife—all because, as Phoebe said later, "you were wearing a skirt."

These are examples of the "inner barriers" to the full participation of women in the life of our church, and of our society. We must be constantly alert to them, because the unequal treatment of women is symptomatic of a much deeper malady. That malady is the refusal to allow human beings to come of age and make their own decisions. In 1867, the philosopher John Stuart Mill said, "The subordination of one sex to another is one of the main obstacles to human progress." This is true in our own families and congregations, in the diocese and national church, and throughout the Anglican Communion and the world.

BEING THE BODY OF CHRIST IN THE WORLD

By 1978, because of my service on the Triennial and the Venture in Mission board, I began to be appointed to represent the Episcopal Church beyond our own borders. I was a delegate to the 1978 Faith and Order Commission of the World Council of Churches in Bangalore, India. I participated in the Partners in Mission consultation with the Nippon

Sei Ko Kai—the Anglican Church in Japan—and later in the Caribbean Conference on Refuges in Belize. I was a delegate to the International Consultation on the Community of Women and Men in the Church, held in Sheffield, England, in 1980.

In 1983, I was one of four Anglicans called to testify on behalf of Bishop Tutu and the South African Council of Churches before the Eloff Commission of Inquiry in South Africa—a truly life-changing experience of the power of faithful Christian witness to stand up to the powers of darkness. As a member of the Anglican Consultative Council, I participated in four of its triennial meetings, in Ontario in 1979, Singapore in 1987, Wales in 1990, and Capetown in 1993. Because of my ACC role, I was one of only nine official women participants in the 1988 Lambeth Conference—alongside over 500 male bishops!

The girl from the mountains of southwest Missouri had begun to see the world! Extraordinary experiences such as these fill me with gratitude and humility, and also some anxiety because I know that I am often seen as a token woman so my "performance" brings credit or blame on all women, not just on myself. At the same time, I have been blessed to gain a much broader view of our church and our world, and of the place of women in them. We are moving steadily into a new vision of humanity and the Body of Christ.

A New Vision of Humanity

It is a vision of women and men committed to the truth of the Gospel, that God created all in the image of God. It is a vision of women and men dedicated to exploring and working toward a new community that celebrates the distinctiveness of each person, male and female. It is a vision which includes helping all persons shed the pressures imposed on himself or herself by oppression, whether it be due to sex, race, class, or sexual orientation—because oppression demeans the oppressor as much as the oppressed. Our goal must be human liberation, so that the relationships of persons and societies are fulfilling for all persons everywhere. There can be no happiness that is lasting and reaches the deepest levels of our being that is based on the suffering or oppression of others.

Our vision, our hope, our prayer is the restoration of all people to unity with God and one another in Christ, and that restoration can come only through the emancipation of all human beings—the oppressed, victims of racism and injustice, the poor, women who are still treated as inferior beings, gay men and lesbians condemned for loving outside the norms, the young who feel they are not being heard, the elderly who are ignored, the handicapped who are overlooked, or church members whose voices are dismissed by their leaders.

This vision of women and men together was, for me, marvelously captured in this quote from the 1982 Pentecost message of the Presidents of the World Council of Churches, one of whom was our own Cynthia Wedel—the first woman to hold that position:

> *An essential part of the Gospel itself is this breaking down of the barriers that so often separate people. Conversion is never merely a religious experience; it is the way in which we become members of that new community where people find their identity in Christ rather than in race, social status or sex. Authentic Christian unity is the fruit of such conversion, the turning of hearts and lives toward God and towards those from whom we are separated.*

My vision—no, my prayer—for the Church in the world as we stand on the brink of a new millenium, is that we will become ever more fully a community of equals ministering in Christ's name to all the world. ✠

DISCOVERING THE EPISCOPAL CHURCH

Bruton Parish Church, Williamsburg, Virginia, February 7, 1999

Many years ago when I was a freshman down the street at William and Mary, a sorority sister from Alpha Chi Omega invited me to come with her to Bruton Parish one morning, and I said 'Yes'. If I had any awareness then of the meaning of "the bondage of our sins" or of the need for salt and savor in my life, it was dim indeed.

I was full of the abundant life of youth, energized by the intellectual stimulation of college, invigorated by the experiences and opportunities of a world so much bigger than the small Missouri town where I grew up. But I came here once, and then again and again. I became active in the Canterbury Club which met before church, at 8 o'clock, every Sunday morning. Eventually I was even teaching Sunday School.

The stately language of the Prayer Book went to my heart. The music and the color and the movement claimed my senses. The preaching of the rector, Francis Craighill, challenged my mind, leading me to recognize issues of life and light, of service and responsibility, of God's claim on my life which I had scarcely thought of before.

I usually sat right up in the balcony, and though I never did sing much myself I loved the way the choir chanted the canticles. Ancient music, the biblical stories of the people of Israel and the followers of Jesus of Nazareth—all these connected me to something much bigger than myself, gave me a place in an enterprise not bound by human limitations.

Most of all, as I learned the faith in this place, I came to know that I didn't need to stay in the flat places of disappointment and failure, the dark places of shame and anger. I found myself called away from all that, called to be filled with saltiness and Light, called to embrace the forgiveness of my sins by our Lord Jesus Christ.

Thanks be to God my friend invited me to Bruton Parish

Church all those years ago. I was confirmed here by Bishop William A. Brown, and certainly never dreamed then of the journey through the organizational channels of the Episcopal Church which lay before me. I would have laughed hysterically had someone said then that I would be elected President of the House of Deputies of the Episcopal Church, a position held 175 years ago by the Rev. William H. Wilmer, Rector of Bruton Parish and President of William and Mary.

To return here today, after being honored at Charter Day at William and Mary yesterday, seems practically unbelievable, a strange and wonderful dream. I'll always feel like a young college student when I stand within these walls—and that's a good thing, I think. It was that young student who heard the call and has done her best to follow Jesus ever since. It's good to come back and reconnect with her now. ♯

A VERY SPECIAL HOMECOMING

Executive Council, Denver, Colorado, February 12, 1999

On a personal note, I'd like to share something quite special that happened this past weekend. Many of you know that I am an alumna of the College of William and Mary in Virginia, and was confirmed at Bruton Parish Church there in Williamsburg. Last Saturday, the College of William and Mary bestowed on me an honorary Doctor of Humane Letters. I was thrilled! And the next morning, at the invitation of the interim rector, Bishop Charles Vache, I preached at Bruton Parish.

Standing there in the pulpit, I remembered myself as an eager young coed being drawn deeper and deeper into the power of the Gospel and the life of the Church. It was an extraordinary experience. I am so deeply grateful to have found my way into the Episcopal Church, and glad that I can share these moments of personal affirmation with you. ♯

THANKSGIVING: LIVING A LIFE OF GRATITUDE

SCHC Companion Conference,
Adelynrood, Byfield, Massachusetts, August 7-11, 1999

The very first position I ever held in the church was as UTO Custodian in my parish. The first time I attended a General Convention, I was there as UTO Custodian of my diocese. The United Thank Offering is surely one of the most remarkable traditions in this church. Think of all those coins dropped with a quick prayer of thanks day after day into that Blue Box on table or bureau—thanksgiving made concrete, solid, tangible.

Think of my little trickle of coins joining those of other women in my parish, and of this growing stream joined with all the others in the diocese, and of our diocesan river flowing with all the other dioceses into a great ocean of thanksgiving. Millions of prayers of thanks made visible, tangible, in millions upon millions of dollars sent into communities around the world, our thank-offerings enabling others to spread the Good News in places we could never go ourselves.

What an excellent lesson in how thanksgiving works, and of how, in community, we can do more than we could ever have imagined. Or rather, God can do more, multiplying our offerings like the loaves and fishes.

CHILDHOOD THANKSGIVINGS

I'd like to share with you several vignettes from my own life which illustrate the development of my understanding about thanksgiving. The first is Thanksgiving itself, Thanksgiving Day, with a capital "T". I worry that much of the original meaning of Thanksgiving Day has been lost in the hubbub of the year's busiest travel holiday and the saccharine coziness of Norman Rockwell.

When I was growing up in the southwest Ozarks, in a multi-generational household headed by my grandfather, Thanksgiving was a very special time indeed. All the relatives gathered at Grandfather's for a great celebration of family, of a bounteous harvest, of the fact that we had come through another year, "Thanks be to God."

Forever associated with those Thanksgiving gatherings, for me, is the first snow of the year. I don't know that it always snowed at Thanksgiving, but it seems that way to me now, and the memory of that first snow is strong: There I am, as a child, looking out the window, as the family gathering hummed along behind me. As clear as day I remember that scene, and the catching of breath that goes with suddenly coming on something wonderful.

I was awestruck by the beauty, black trees against the white, big flakes drifting lazily down, the anticipation of wetness on my cheeks and the crunch of snow under my boots when we were allowed to venture outside after dinner.

Women and Children Last

Now I must tell you about one aspect of those Thanksgiving gatherings that I did not feel thankful for then, and still remember with annoyance. We were a large family on those occasions, so we couldn't all fit around the dining room table. This is true for many families, so the children eat at the kitchen table, or a second table is set up in the living room or in the front hallway, or whatever.

My family solved the problem this way: the men ate first. Then, the women cleared the table, washed the dishes, reset the table, and only then finally got to eat, after working in the kitchen since early morning. I didn't quite understand what was going on, but I didn't like it then, and today I am only a little bit grateful that my consciousness began to be raised so many years ago!

AUNT BESS

Another aspect of my childhood that relates to gratitude and thankfulness is my Aunt Bess. She was 17 years older than my mother, and had been widowed at the age of 23. She never married again, and lived with us in Grandfather's crowded house, where I shared a bed with her every night as I was growing up. She was a wonderful woman, more like a grandmother than an aunt, who told me stories about Hiawatha and many other tales that I begged to hear again and again.

She was, I suppose, the greatest influence on my life—and she was a woman of deep faith. I still have a book my mother gave her at Easter in 1952, Diary of Private Prayer, by John Bailley. Mother inscribed it as follows: "Nobody will enjoy these prayers so well as you, for you are the most unselfish and God-like person I have ever known." I treasure that book, because it was a gift to Aunt Bess from my mother, and a powerful symbol of the interrelatedness of the three of us.

Aunt Bess was an extraordinary blessing in my life. As I think back on all the time we shared, the values she taught me by example, her unselfishness, her love, I am filled with thankfulness. This wonderful woman powerfully influenced who I am and I could never fully have thanked her for what she did. How much more thankful must I be, then, to the God who created me and blessed my life with the presence of Aunt Bess.

When we are blessed with a situation which elicits deep gratitude toward another person, we have an opportunity to learn more about what it means to be grateful to God. So it was with Aunt Bess. I often remember my Uncle Dewey, her brother, saying that she was his proof that there is a God.

GOD'S CALL AND MOONLIGHT

God's call is renewed again and again, in so many different ways, when I have the eyes to see and ears to hear. The call can come concretely, tangibly, like coins in a Blue Box. It may come in words on a page of Scripture, or in a hymn or prayer, or from the heart and mind of a friend. Often it comes through moments of such unexpected beauty that you want to point and share: "Look! How wonderful!"—like that first snow at Thanksgiving, or the rising of the moon.

I have a place down on the river in Irvington, Virginia, with a dock stretching out over the water. It is a favorite place to sit in the evening, to watch the sun go down. Once there was a full moon, as we sat out there at the end of the dock. As it rose, it threw a great pathway of shimmering light across the water, so magnificent that there were no words to convey either its beauty or my deep sense of awe and gratitude.

Back in Missouri, when the moon came up over the mountain, there were times when it seemed to hang there so close to earth that I thought I could reach out and touch it. More than once I thought, "I'm really going to hate to die, because I won't see the moon coming up anymore." ✠